SEEKING THE LOST, KEEPING THEM, MAKING THEM DISCIPLES:

Transforming New Converts from Members to Disciples
Through a Christ-Based Discipleship Program

by Dr. Benoit Petit-Homme

DORRANCE
PUBLISHING CO
EST. 1920
PITTSBURGH, PENNSYLVANIA 15238

Dorrance Publishing Co
585 Alpha Drive
Pittsburgh, PA 15238
Visit our website at *www.dorrancebookstore.com*

ISBN: 978-1-4809-5896-8
eISBN: 978-1-4809-5919-4

TABLE OF CONTENTS

SECTION IV: THE PROGRAM [TRANSFORMING NEW CONVERTS FROM MEMBERS TO DISCIPLES]

BONUS: THE ULTIMATE COMEBACK

FOREWORD

As Christ locked eyes with his followers while telling them, that sharing the message of God's love with every member of the human race, as a witness to the entire world, it would seem impossible for them to achieve. Accomplishing this was simply not possible for human beings to conceive. After Jesus rose from the grave, the believers who were faithful to him were just a few hundred in number. How would this modest-sized group of believers reach a generation of suspicious and stubborn followers if Jesus had labored for three and one half years with such a limited return on His efforts?

Christ conveyed what we know as the Gospel Commission. This exhortation to the Christian church admonishes us to teach, preach, baptize, and make disciples of people. Accompanying this exhortation is the promise that He would be with us in this missional work until the end of the age.

In this post-modern and post-Christian age with its rapidly expanding world population fostered by seemingly insurmountable obstacles facing the church in its task of sharing Christ with the world, this mission seems humanly impossible. With each beat of the human heart, there is a new birth into existence. The world's population doubles every twenty years. Amazingly, despite the combustible growth in population we experience declining and diminishing membership of Christian churches. As church attendance is sliding, sports arenas are filling up with fans who quest for larger facilities to accommodate additional people.

Seeking the Lost, Keeping Them, Making Them Disciples by Dr. Benoit Petit-Homme is a handy Christ-based discipleship resource that will contribute to the mission of training and equipping church ministry leaders in the evangelistic work of reaping, retaining, and nurturing new believing Christians. This is a must-read for church officers, pastors and ministry directors in the Christian church.

Ron C. Smith, PhD., D.Min,
President, Southern Union Conference of SDA

PREFACE

In the month of April 1994, my home church conducted a huge evangelistic series on the Book of Revelation. As a result of this gospel outreach, two hundred and fifty-three people got baptized and accepted Christ as their Personal Savior. However, it did not take long to discover that over seventy-five percent of the new believers had left the church in less than six months.

Being a member of the visitations committee gave me the opportunity to meet with these neophytes who had become very hostile to the gospel. It was an appalling experience to know that several of them abandoned the church due to lack of spiritual maturity. Greatly disturbed by this early exit that has been also surveyed in many other Adventist congregations throughout the past twenty years, I felt compelled to write this book to help new converts build and develop a lasting, loving relationship with Jesus. Conversing with so many of them and listening carefully to their stories made me confident that the believers can be transformed from simply church members to devoted Disciples of Christ.

"*Seeking the Lost, Keeping Them, and Making Them Disciples*" is mainly about passionately sharing the gospel with the unsaved, lovingly retaining them, and patiently equipping them for ministry to fulfill the Great Commission. It also provides ten universal, biblical principles for a successful evangelism strategy, and seven critical keys for retaining the new believers before their initiation to the discipleship world. To pass up the challenge of the early exit in the church, "*Seeking the Lost…*" proposes a ten-week Christ-Centered discipleship program that furthers their training and facilitates their assimilation in their community of faith.

Getting information from those who had left the church was not an easy task. However, with tact, love, patience, and the cooperation of the Holy Spirit, these people played a critical role in the realization of this endeavor as they gave the reasons for leaving their congregations. They were practically my primary sources of contact to gather statistical data to prepare the discipleship program. Throughout the process of writing this book, I became more and more cognizant of the necessity for the church to be intentional in making discipleship an integrant part of its tenets.

"*Seeking the Lost…*" is a general wake-up call for those who call themselves Christ's friends and followers and have a passion for the souls. It unequivocally shows in its bonus chapter that the events that must precede Christ's Second Coming are literally being fulfilled daily. Christ's true and obedient followers must be at work day and night to respond to Jesus' mandate, which is to make disciples. Jesus is coming soon to take His faithful disciples home and live with them forever. Thus, let us all enroll in Christ's Discipleship School!

"*Seeking the Lost…*" could not have become a finished product without the sustenance and the guidance of the Almighty God. First of all, I want to praise His name and thank Him for all the success. Secondly, I am especially grateful to my wife, Carolle, and my two sons, Carl and Berny, for their unconditional love and support during all the phases that have led to the completion of this project. Thirdly, my gratitude goes to my extended family, siblings, and in-laws who have been very supportive of me. Fourthly, I am indebted to all the pastors who have invited me into their churches where I was able to test the feasibility of the discipleship program described in this book.

I would like to thank Dr. Edward Schmidt, Director of the North American Division Evangelism Institute (NADEI) for inviting me as a guest lecturer for the "Church Growth and the Equipping Pastor" course at Andrews University in the context of this project. In particular, I would like to thank Dr. Jeanette Bryson, PhD., Chair, Education Department at Washington Adventist University for reading the manuscript and making sound suggestions.

Among many others, such as Dr. Jason Vickers, PhD., my mentor, my indebtedness goes to Dr. Kathleen Beagles, PhD, then professor at Andrews University, who had made me become more and more appreciative of discipleship due to her powerful insights on the topic.

I would like to express my gratitude to the editorial, production, and marketing teams at Dorrance Publishing Company, Inc. for the substantial time and talents that they have given to this project. Last, but not definitely least, I am particularly grateful to Mr. John Rectenwald at Dorrance Publishing Company, Inc. for promptly initiating the editing process of this book.

Once again, to the Almighty God belongs all the glory!

Dr. Benoit Petit-Homme
Fall 2017

INTRODUCTION

Upon receiving her federal income tax refund check, a woman ran to an appliance store to buy a refrigerator. On her way back home, she stopped at a supermarket to buy groceries. She then filled the fridge with vegetables, meat, fruit, and so on. A couple days later, she smelt a bad odor and discovered that her stuff was spoiled. Angry, she quickly called the store to tell them to come take the fridge back because it was not working. The store manager sent a technician on the spot, who found out that there was nothing wrong with the refrigerator. The only problem was that the fridge was not connected to the power line. Was there anything wrong with the fridge? No. What went wrong with the fridge? It was not connected to the power line. Could the fridge connect itself to the power line? No. Who should have connected it to the power line? The woman should have.

Making disciples of all nations constitutes one of the greatest assignments that Jesus bestowed upon His disciples before ascending to heaven. In other words, the biblical imperative set by the Master is to make disciples. Unfortunately, instead of making disciples as stated by Christ, the church seems inclined to making members. Rounding up people and getting them to join the church does not finish the task that Jesus commanded. This alarming situation leads to low retention and huge dropouts of new converts. Several denominational Churches have been facing the challenge of simply making members for years. They have failed to assimilate those who have been won for Christ. These churches too often equate baptism of new converts to the end of their spiritual journey and overlook Jesus' command of making disciples. As a result, the percentage of new converts leaving the church shortly after baptism due to lack of Christian maturity and inactivity is considerably high. For instance, a survey conducted by the Center for Creative Ministry in May 2013 for the Office of Archives, Statistics, and Research of General Conference of Seventh-day Adventists, has reported that 70 percent of church dropouts are found among the converted to the Church.[i]

In the story mentioned in the beginning, the fridge can be compared to the new believers, the woman to the church at large and leadership team in particular, and the power line to Jesus Christ. For over twenty-two years, I have met and heard several new converts explaining why they have not become involved or participated in church activities and left the church shortly after baptism. I have randomly questioned several of them and got different answers. However, I have grouped the reasons given into ten main categories. For the sake of this study, emphasis will be put on the first five groups surveyed with a higher repeated frequency. Firstly, they did not feel loved enough after their conversion. Secondly, they did not understand very well the decision made. Thirdly, they did not know how to share their new belief. Fourthly, they were not adequately trained to minister to others. And fifthly, they did not really have friends in the new community.

According to the story told above, these five categories (Love, Understanding of God's Word, Ministering, Equipping, and Networking: LUMEN) can be replaced by a single word, which is Connection. If they are not connected to Jesus Christ, new believers will find all kinds of excuses to not become involved in the life of the church and refuse to become a disciple. In fact, we have never seen a three-month-old babe feeding themselves, or a one-year old child going to school alone. They need someone to lead them. Likewise, being babes in faith (1 Pt 2: 2), new converts cannot at first connect themselves to Christ. Like the fridge, they need others to help them connect to Christ. It is the church's duty to do so. Connection to the Savior is not an easy task, but it is not impossible either. This connection can be traced from Jesus' way and methodology of making disciples. It thus can be reached when new believers are transformed from simply church members to Disciples of Christ as stated in the Great Commission.

The non-involvement of new converts in church activities due to lack of maturity in their relationship with Christ creates the necessity for a Christ-based discipleship model that is biblically rooted, historically sound, and theologically relevant for new converts. Transitioning new believers from members to disciples is at the heart of the Great Commission. Understanding the necessity and the importance of that transition, Thayer rightly writes, "If we do not have a plan to disciple the new converts, we may inoculate them against Christianity. They will live for a while in the wonder of Christ's grace and love, but may stumble in their walk with the Master when temptations, troubles, and then doubts attack them. Led to accept Christ as their Savior, but too often, no one is guiding them in their walk with Him as their Lord. If they drop out of their early walk with Christ, they may be resistant to new appeals to follow Christ."[1]

The purpose of this volume is to propose a Christ-based discipleship program that can facilitate this transition and help new converts to build a constant, personal, and spiritual relationship with Jesus. "Transforming New Converts from Members to Disciples" seeks also to tackle the issue of non-involvement of new converts through active participation in church affairs and ministry. The goal is to move new converts from being simple religious consumers to healthy and productive disciples like Christ. Discipleship implies engagement and action; it is perhaps in that context that Hawkins writes, "To be a disciple of Jesus means inviting others to look with the eyes of faith so that they too see this already present community and reorder their lives in response to its presence."[2]

Transforming new converts from members to disciples is in line with the Master's final Great Commission. "Making disciples was the prevailing passion and top priority of Christ in order to proliferate his gospel, and that must be our passion and priority as well."[3] The main job of the church consists of making disciples. In other words, every church should be a training school for Christian workers. This idea of training church members to become engaged disciples in the vineyard of the Master is well expressed by one of the Adventist pioneer writers as follows: "The greatest help that can be given our people is to teach them to work for God, and depend on him, not on the minister."[4]

Making disciples requires intentionality and a clear comprehension of God's mission that is materialized in the person of His Son, Jesus-Christ. God's mission has always been throughout the biblical history the salvation of the lost human race. This was Jesus' clear mission statement:

"For the Son of Man came to seek and to save the lost (Luke 19:10)." Christ has called all of us, His disciples, to join Him in His mission of seeking and saving the lost. To fulfill that mission, we must be intentional in seeking the lost in utilizing Christ's methodology, keeping them and making them disciples of Christ. New converts should and will not stay babes forever. They need to grow and become mature so they can, at their turn, make disciples as well. This growth is possible through earnest prayer, Bible study, witnessing, and a vital connection to Christ who has begun the good work in them (Ph 1: 6; 1 Th 5: 24) and will strengthen them (Ph 4: 13). As we are nearing Christ's Second Coming, we must more than ever feel compelled to fulfill the Great Commission. This will become a reality through the preaching of the gospel (Mt 24: 14) in partnership with the Holy Spirit (Ac 1: 8). Disciples are called, chosen, and commissioned to preach the good news (Mt 28: 19). Thus, the church is called not to make members but rather disciples accordingly with Christ's final command to the eleven and to us as well.

Even though discipling others or making disciples is not an easy enterprise, this volume will help the reader discover that it is feasible and doable in cooperation with the Holy Spirit. Keep in mind that we are unable to perform this task alone, but rather with the empowerment of the Holy Spirit that Jesus had promised. It is thus impossible for Jesus (God) to lie (He 6: 18). Christ, to whom nothing is impossible (Lk 1: 37) and who says that He will be with us in the making of disciples until the end of the ages (Mt 28: 19, 20), will certainly keep His words. The assurance of Christ's presence in this endeavor seems to be intentionally reported by Matthew. He indeed began his gospel with Immanuel, God with us, (Mt 1: 21) and concluded it with similar thought, "And surely I (Jesus) am with you always, to the very end of the age (Mt 28: 20b)."

The following sections and chapters outline the cursory look leading to the Christ-based discipleship program described in this manual:

Section I, comprising of chapters one, two, and three, sets the theoretical framework of this project and gives the biblical, historical, and theological foundations of discipleship.

Section II, containing chapters four, five, and six, displays the heart of this study: seeking the lost (Evangelism), keeping them (Retention), and discipling them (Discipleship).

Section III, comprising of chapters seven, eight, and nine, provides a succinct survey of literature selected aiding in the preparation of materials, focuses on the research method used highlighting the research design, instruments, and measurement tools for evaluating the program, and underlines the preparatory works leading to the realization of the program.

Section IV, containing chapters ten, eleven, and twelve, presents the Christ-based discipleship program and its implementation providing the results of the field experience through collection, analysis and interpretation of data collected. It provides reflections, considerations, and the conclusion.

A bonus chapter (13), which is an outline of the "Blessed Hope" of all Christ's disciples, is also provided to emphasize the importance of the Second Coming of Jesus and encourage them to get ready to receive their reward from the Master.

May the reading of this volume help you discover that discipleship is all about Love (Agape), self-sacrifice, love for God, and love for our neighbors!

1: Jane Thayer, *Teaching for Discipleship: Strategies for Transformational Learning* (Unpublished, 2009), 2.

2: Thomas R. Hawkins, *Cultivating Christian Community* (Nashville, TN: Discipleship Resources, 2001), 26.

3: Philip G. Samaan, *Christ's Way of Making Disciples* (Hagerstown, MD: Review and Herald Publishing Association, 1999), 13.

4: Ellen G. White, *Christian Service* (Hagerstown, MD: Review and Herald Publishing Association, 2002), 58.

CHAPTER ONE
BIBLICAL FOUNDATION OF DISCIPLESHIP

It is true that the word *discipleship* is not found in the Bible. However, there is no doubt that this concept can be traced from a biblical stance. When we consider Moses' relationship with Joshua and some of his elders, the liaison between Elijah and Elisha in the Old Testament, and Jesus' ministry in the New Testament, we can boldly say that discipleship constitutes a biblical model. Indeed, the ministry of the apostle Paul and Timothy represents an irrefutable proof that the Bible teaches and values discipleship.

Toward a Biblical Understanding of the Word Discipleship/Disciple
Like the word *Trinity* and other biblical terms, the word discipleship is alluded to in Scripture. In this case, Diop has rightly written, "The concept of discipleship expresses the most profound conceivable relationship and allegiance according to Jesus' own statements in the Gospels. The most urgent need of the church is not only to make converts but to make disciples. Converts can leave the church as they come in. Disciples display an unswerving allegiance to Jesus that nothing can deter."[1] This statement illustrates that the most common word derived from discipleship is *disciple*. Continuing his word origin analysis, Diop adds that "The English word disciple is borrowed from the Latin discipulus, itself derived from dissipere, to grasp intellectually. Etymologically, the word disciple, in Greek mathetes, is derived from the root math and is connected to the concept of learner, pupil, follower, or apprentice. The

word disciple is connected to the idea of learning."[2] Joshua and Elisha were not called disciples but rather servants; however, both learned from their masters, Moses and Elijah respectively, and had to continue and sometimes reproduce their works (Josh 1: 1, 2; 1 Kg 2: 1-12).

Thus, it is easy to note the biblical origin of the term discipleship. According to Del Dunavant, "The word disciple is used in the Bible over 264 times, depending upon the translation."[3] Concluding his word study, he indicates that "a believer is a disciple as soon as she follows Jesus, as soon as he accepts God's gift of eternal life. You do not become a disciple only after you have learned to be good enough! Discipleship is, however, a lifelong process."[4] Among many others, two scriptural passages from the Old and New Testament have been selected to lay the biblical foundation of discipleship. The first text is taken from Exodus 18: 17-20, and the second from Matthew 28: 16-20.

Old Testament
Though discipleship is not found in the Old Testament, the word disciple appears in a few references. The prophet Isaiah, making use of it in the eighth chapter of his book, writes: "Bind up the testimony, seal the law among my disciples (Is 8: 16)." In the New Testament, Mark reports that Jesus called the twelve to become His disciples:" When He had called the people to Himself, with His disciples also, He said to them, ""Whoever desires to come after me, let him deny himself, and take up his cross, and follow me. For whoever desires to save his life will lose it; but whoever loses his life for my sake and the gospel's will save it! (Mk 8: 34, 35)."Moses mentions that God did the same in the Old Testament with Abraham, "Now the LORD had said to Abram: Get out of your country, from your family and from your father's house, to a land that I will show you (Gn 12: 1)" and his descendants (Am 3: 1-3). Jesus wanted His disciples to become like Him, "If you keep My commandments, you will abide in My love, just as I have kept My Father's commandments and abide in His love (Jn 15: 10);" God is holy and desired the same thing for the Israelite people, "For I am the LORD who brings you up out of the land of Egypt, to be your God. You shall therefore be holy, for I am holy (Le 11: 45)." These few passages among many others show without ambiguity the allusion to discipleship in the Old Testament.

Exodus 18 can be divided into two big sections. In part one (18:1-12), one witnesses Jethro's acknowledgment of the God of Moses:" The word of Yahweh's victory over Egypt has spread so as to reach Jethro's ears. Unlike the nations of 15:14-16 who tremble at such news, Jethro is attracted to it, and so he comes to Moses."[5] The focus for this project is on the second part (18:13-27) that has reported Jethro's advice to Moses in particular verses 17-20. It makes no doubt that "verses 13-27 center on community structures that give shape to the life of faith."[6]

""You are not acting wisely, his father-in-law replied. ""You will surely wear yourself out, and not only yourself but also these people with you. The task is too heavy for you; you cannot do it alone. Now, listen to me, and I will give you some advice, that God may be with you. Act as the people's representative before God, bringing to him whatever they have to say. Enlighten them in regard to the decisions and regulations, showing them how they are to live and what they are to do"" (Ex 18: 17-20).

Structure, Literary and Historical Context

In considering the literary and traditio-historical analysis of the whole chapter, one does not observe much discrepancy among the scholars. This point is clearly elucidated by Childs in his book: "There is general agreement among critical scholars that chapter 18 is basically a unified narrative. Attempts, such as that of Gressmann, to find two complete strands have remained extremely unconvincing. Only occasionally are there signs of duplication."[7]

It becomes obvious to discover that there is a historical dimension to the second part of the chapter as it is expressed by Childs: "A whole series of historical changes in Israel's legal system structure are mirrored in the story through the variety of vocabulary used as well as in the concepts of the Mosaic office. When one turns to the second part, interest is focused immediately on the details of the new judicial organization. Interest focused on understanding how the early judges performed their duties, such as delegating the legal responsibility through the proper channels, and the like. Christian biblical scholars continued very much along the same lines."[8] In addition to its historical dimension, the second section of the chapter presents another societal aspect of the organization of the Jewish people in the wilderness that is clearly explained by George Arthur Buttrick: "The civil organization of Israel's society in a later day was founded by Moses, under Jethro's instruction. The account is both etiological and historical in purpose. In Numbers 11:11-17, 24-30, later followed by the Deuteronomist (Dt 1:9-18), Moses himself is said to have found the burden of his work too heavy; and the foundation of the more differentiated administration is represented as having ordained by God, without any reference to Jethro."[9]

The immediate literary context found in the text leads to the necessity of a discipleship program. Douglas makes a clear description of the problem in the following statement.

Exodus 18:13 pictures a lamentable situation. Now came a day when Moses could wait no longer to address the caseload, and in spite of spending all daylight hours hearing court cases, he had apparently not finished when evening came. Jethro saw that this could not go on indefinitely. His own experience as a Midianite leader may have involved him in regular judging among the Midianites, and it was obvious to him that Moses had overcommitted his time to his judicial role. Nothing was wrong with Moses' serving as a judge; instead it was clearly an obligation of his as leader of the people. What was wrong was his serving as the only judge, without any help, for simple cases as well as for complex ones.[10]

Theology, Message and Contemporary Significance
In Exodus 18. 17-18, Jethro did not find Moses' methodical process of judging the people persuasive and overcame it with a clear and sound proposition. He encouraged his son-in-law to adopt a more convenient and appropriate method that would benefit everyone. After spending so many years in the Egyptian bondage, the Israelites had lost the sense of living in a friendly community. Several of them became upset and frustrated when they could not be served or heard in due time. Jethro discovered that Moses' judicial workload could not be the activity of a single individual. It was necessary for the God-appointed leader to have other trained leaders to help him perform the task; in other words, Moses had to coach more devoted men to help him share the load. There is a critical spiritual take-out that can be drawn from the text: "Stop criticizing church leaders, but rather offer to them good advice." Jethro did not undermine Moses' managerial abilities; he simply pointed out the problem, and carefully proposed a solution.

The advice Jethro gives is a much-needed remedy to a problematic situation. It is still relevant to today's church. One of the main reasons new converts leave the church is a lack of knowledge. The ministers mostly see themselves, as ministers only, and take upon themselves all of the responsibilities. Not only do they kill themselves, but also they do not have time to properly feed the flock. Even though they have good intention, it is impossible for them to be able to do everything at the same time. Through Jethro's advice to Moses, one can understand that it is not God's intention to give just one person the responsibility and the care of His people.

In fact, in Numbers 11: 10-15 is recorded what R. Allen calls Moses' lament. In this passage, one can witness Moses' complaint about the people: "He realized that the burden was too demanding and he could not manage all these people alone. Moses was distressed as he found the assignment too heavy for him. Moses was incensed at the people for making his role as a leader an unbearable one and toward Yahweh for assigning him this overwhelming burden of leadership. His reaction is pointed primarily toward God, challenging the divine decision to place him in the parental role of providing for this nation."[11]

The passage makes clear that God acknowledged Moses' request to have helpers in leading the people. Numbers 11:16-17 clearly depicts Yahweh's reply to Moses as Cole wrote it: "The Lord instructed Moses to appoint seventy elders from among the leaders who were also officers among the Israelites. The Hebrew term soter ('official' or 'scribal assistant') suggests a kind of official with scribal function within a given group. Moses' role was to gather the seventy elders and present them before the Lord at the entrance to the Tent of Meeting, the standard place for revelatory activity from the Lord and where priests and Levites were anointed and commissioned for service."[12] At this point, it is interesting to note that the Lord would impart to these elders some of His spirit that had already been poured out upon Moses.

In carefully reading Exodus 18:19-20, one can easily identify the concept of discipleship. Douglas helps us understand Jethro's advice to Moses as God's initiation and confirmation to discipleship in stating that "Jethro did not suggest that Moses discontinue judging, or that he stop serving as a representative of the people's problems to God, or that he leave off being God's spokesperson to teach the people God's decrees and laws. The people surely needed someone to show them the way to live and the duties they are to perform, and Moses was indeed that person. Moreover, Jethro did not arrogate to himself divine wisdom but was careful to couch his words as suggestions subject to God's confirmation."[13] Furthermore, describing Moses' responsibility, Ronald E. Clements, in his commentary on verse 20, wrote: "You must instruct them. All the people were to be taught the basic contents of case law, and this teaching would normally be carried out in the context of family life."[14] A critical reading of Exodus 18:24-26 gives assumption that the plan works well. Jethro's advice to Moses can be seen as God's command. This principle of dividing labor has set the growth of the early church as it is reported in Acts 6: 1-6.

The biblical model found in the Old Testament (Ex 18: 13-27) shows clearly that the pastor has the responsibility to prepare others to lead. The most important job of the minister is not preaching but training others to ease the burden. Once they are well trained and equipped, these disciples will be able to teach new converts. As they become more knowledgeable about God's love and church's policies, they will remain in the church to joyfully serve the Lord.

Exodus 18: 13-27 presents a plain narrative. There is more in the passage than a simple story where Moses' father-in-law provides him with some counsel. It is thus plausible to see a certain divine wisdom behind Jethro's advice. After so many years of Egyptian bondage, the people had lost the sense of living in a friendly environment. It appeared vital that Moses instructed them to settle their disputes. However, it was obvious that he could not do this burdensome work alone. He had to have helpers. As they join the church, new converts do not know much about their new faith. It is up to the pastor to make disciples to tell and teach them so they also become disciples rather than being simply members.

New Testament
If the word disciple is rarely found in the Old Testament, the situation is different in the New Testament. It becomes a dominant term in the four gospels and the book of Acts. Baker's evangelical dictionary of theology gives a very relational definition of the term: "The characteristic name for those who gathered around Jesus during his ministry was disciple. He was the teacher or master; they were his disciples (mathētai), a term involving too much personal attachment and commitment to be adequately rendered by pupil. The name

was carried over into Acts, where it frequently has the general sense of Christian (cf. Acts 14:21)."[14]

The New Testament biblical passage chosen for the support of this project was Matthew chapter 28 verses 16-20. However, because it contains the greatest assignment that Jesus had given his disciples before ascending to heaven, verse 19 is the main point of focus.

The eleven disciples went to Galilee, to the mountain to which Jesus had ordered them. When they saw him, they worshiped, but they doubted. Then Jesus approached and said to them, "All power in heaven and on earth has been given to me. Go, therefore, and make disciples of all nations, baptizing them in the name of the Father, and of the Son, and of the Holy Spirit, teaching them to observe all that I have commanded you. And behold, I am with you always, until the end of the age" (Mt 28: 18-20).

Matthew 28: 16-20 is generally called the Great Commission. It contains the final instructive words from Jesus to His disciples. Craig L. Blomberg, summarizing this passage, wrote, "This short account contains the culmination and combination of all of Matthew's central themes: (1) the move from particularism to universalism in the preaching of the gospel of the kingdom; (2) discipleship and the establishment of the church; (3) Jesus' commands as ultimately incumbent on Christians; and (4) the abiding present of Jesus as teacher, as divine Son of God, and the risen and Sovereign Lord of the universe."[15] It is also noteworthy to read the comment of T. R. France on this fundamental passage:

> "This final short paragraph plays a crucial role, which justifies its being set apart as a final main section of the narrative structure. In these few words, many of the most central themes of the gospel reach their resolution and culmination. The preparation of the twelve as Jesus' task force, which had apparently ended in irreversible disaster in 26:56, is now resumed as they (or rather eleven of them) are restored to their position of trust and responsibility and given the final instructions for fulfilling the mission for which they were originally called in 10:1-15."[16]

Moreover, the writer furthers his theological and biblical analysis when using the passage to establish the link existing between discipleship in the Old Testament and in the New Testament. He even tries to remove several doubts about the insertion or inclusion of this biblical concept in the Old Testament. The following statement makes the case of his argument:

"Jesus' assignment to the disciples in Matthew 28:19-20 represents the ideal of discipleship in the Old Testament. The covenantal relationship that God had with Israel should be extended to the other nations through Israel's witnessing. Since they have failed in their mission Jesus reiterates it to the eleven and per extension to each and every one. Jesus' final words in the Gospel of Matthew are often referred to as the Great Commission, and scholars have pointed out how closely this scene resembles, in its overall sense and content if not in detail, the commission narratives which occur throughout the Old Testament where God's often reluctant and inadequate servants are sent out to fulfill his purpose with the assurance of his empowering and his presence to go with them; such stories are told notably of Abraham, Moses, Joshua, Gideon, Samuel, Isaiah, and Jeremiah. Such stories mark the beginning, not the end, of that person's service, and this is how it is here for the disciples."[17]

A church should not be reluctant in proclaiming the good news. The One who has sent his people possesses all the power they need to accomplish this task. In other words, He has been given all (universal) authority in heaven and on earth. One must understand that making disciples is not a suggestion or an optional matter. It is rather a mandatory and divine requirement. This assignment was given by the risen Savior, the King of kings.

> "Before formally giving them the Great Commission, Jesus assures the disciples he has the power to do so. It was a reassurance because, when he sent the seventy out, they testified that the Devil has submitted to them in the name of Jesus. In his earthly ministry Jesus had declared his authority as the Son of Man to forgive sin (Matthew 9:6) and to reveal the Father (11:26). Now as the risen Messiah he has been given all authority, glory, and power, who is rightly worshipped by all peoples and nations and whose dominion and kingdom last forever (Dan.7:13-14)."[18]

Matthew 28:16-20 can be viewed as a summary of the whole Gospel. Jesus appears as the risen Lord who is worthy to be approached in an attitude of homage or worship. The teacher par excellence commissions his disciples to carry on his teaching and also affirms that all authority has been given to him. The passage clearly puts emphasis on discipleship, as verse 19 shows unequivocally the duty and responsibility of the church.

Bloomberg, in the following statement, helps grasp a better understanding of Jesus' final order to His followers:

> "The main command of Christ's commission is make disciples (matheteusate). To make disciples of all nations does not require many people to leave their homelands, but Jesus' main focus remains on the task of all believers to duplicate themselves wherever they may be. The commission is expressed not in terms of the means, to proclaim the good news, but of the end, to make disciples. It is not enough that the nations hear the message; they must also respond with the same commitment, which was required of those who became disciples of Jesus during his terrestrial ministry. The verb make disciples also commands a kind of evangelism that does not stop after someone makes a profession of faith. The truly subordinate participles in v.19 explain what making disciples involves, baptizing them and teaching them obedience to all of Jesus' commandments. The first of these will be a once-for-all, decisive initiation into Christian community. The second proves a perennially incomplete, life-long task."[19]

It is interesting to comprehend the meaning of the text. The disciples are commissioned to make disciples of all nations (panta ta ethne), not to simply make church members. One of the reasons new converts leave the church is the fact that they are not taught. Baptism without further instruction is not sufficient to keep someone in church or make that person a disciple. It is time for the church to stop considering baptism as the end of the Christian journey. It must rather be seen as the beginning. After choosing His disciples, Jesus took much time to teach them. He invested His time, ideas, and efforts in them in order to equip them for the work. His personality was so reflected in these disciples that even the critics who accused them had to acknowledge the fact that they were with Jesus (Acts 4:13). They followed and observed attentively the Master before He sent them out to do missionary work. Jesus used a model of constant repetition to instruct His followers. He taught them the importance to study the word and remain in contact with the Father through prayer.

Teaching obedience to all of Jesus' commands forms the heart of disciple making. The apostle Paul, understanding the importance of teaching, invites Timothy, his young partner in ministry, to do so. "Command and teach these things (1 Ti 4:11)." The teaching part of the Great Commission has been neglected for too long. This is why so many new converts leave the church after a short period of their conversion. If teaching was not so critical, Jesus would not ask His disciples to do so. God has always wanted His people to know much more about Him. And this can be done only through sound biblical teaching. Commenting on Matthew 28:20 about the teaching part of the Great Commission, Craig L. Blomberg writes, "Jesus' words further demonstrate that Christian ethics and morality should first of all focus on Jesus' teaching, even though the Old Testament still remains relevant, as one sees how it is fulfilled in Christ (Mt 5:17-20), and even though the rest of the Testament remains relevant as further explanation of Christ and his teachings."[20]

The same Jesus who commanded the making of disciples and the baptizing of them is the one who ordered the teaching of those who would accept the message. Teaching is so crucial that it has a double appearance in the passage. An individual would not ask for baptism without being aware of what baptism is. It is through teaching that someone can know about repentance that leads to baptism. The true knowledge about God is generally gained through teaching after baptism. To remain in church and become disciples making disciples for the kingdom of God, new converts need to be taught. It is a principle traced from the Old Testament, emphasized by Jesus, and correctly applied by the apostles including the apostle Paul.

Finally, a careful reading of Matthew 28:16-20 will allow us to discover the most important themes of the Gospel, such as, convincing the Jewish people that Christ was the promised Messiah. The passage clearly shows that the Father has given Jesus supreme and universal authority. Christ, on His part, has given the Great Commission to His followers. The disciples are to share their discipleship not only with their fellow Jews, but also with all the nations. It is evident that discipleship does not stop at baptism but continues on with solid biblical teachings. Teaching is so critical that Jesus promised that the Father would send His substitute teacher after His departure: "But the Helper, the Holy Spirit, whom the Father will send in my name, he will teach you all things and bring to your remembrance all that I have said to you (Jn14:26)." The biblical principle is that new converts need to become disciples. They should be taught while they grow into a fully devoted follower of Jesus. They then must be equipped to introduce their best friend, Jesus, to others.

Conclusion

Both the Old and the New Testaments value discipleship. When a church neglects discipleship, its membership will soon or later decline toward death. Discipleship really matters since it has been modeled and commanded by Jesus. When a church does not value discipleship, they automatically undermine the importance of the Great Commission. When a church does not practice discipleship, they reject the Lordship of Jesus who unequivocally gave the mandate to make disciples of all nations (Mt 28: 19). A congregation that is not interested in making disciples is a rebellious and disobedient assembly that will disappear soon. A church minimizing discipleship is unable to totally reflect or reveal Christ's character to the perishing and His loving mission to save the lost. When a church forsakes discipleship, most of its new converts will soon give up on faith, and will be easily swept away by false doctrines. Biblical discipleship helps to avoid confusion, laziness, and complacency among the followers of Christ. Biblical discipleship motivates Christ's followers to share the good news and haste the Second Coming (Mt 24:14). To reach out for spiritual growth and fulfill Jesus' mission, the church needs to involve new converts in ministries through an effective Christ-based discipleship model. Christ is coming soon. It is the time right now to profusely write and talk about discipleship, and also to implement it in the life of the church.

1: Ganoune Diop, *Make Disciples: The Art of Moving Beyond Conversion to a Passion for Christ* (Huntsville, AL: Oakwood College Press, 2010),

2: Ganoune Diop, *Make Disciples: The Art of Moving Beyond Conversion to a Passion for Christ* (Huntsville, AL: Oakwood College Press, 2010), 5-6.

3: Del Dunavant, *From Membership to Discipleship: A Practical Guide to Equipping Members for Ministry* (Lincoln, NE: AdventSource, 2006), 54.

4: Del Dunavant, *From Membership to Discipleship: A Practical Guide to Equipping Members for Ministry* (Lincoln, NE: AdventSource, 2006), 54.

5: Peter Enns, "Exodus" *The NIV Application Commentary* (Grand Rapids, MI: Zondervan Publishing House, 2000), 367.

6: Terence E. Fretheim, *Exodus Interpretation, A Bible Commentary for Teaching and Preaching* (Louisville, KY: John Knox Press, 1991), 195.

7: Brevard S. Childs, *The Book of Exodus, A Critical, Theological Commentary* (Philadelphia, PA: The Westminster Press, 1974), 321.

8: Brevard S. Childs, *The Book of Exodus, A Critical, Theological Commentary* (Philadelphia, PA: The Westminster Press, 1974), 333-334.

9: George Arthur Buttrick, *The Interpreter's Bible, vol.1* (Nashville, TN: Abingdon Press, 1980), 966.

10: Douglas K. Stuart, "Exodus," *The New American Commentary, vol. 2* (Nashville, TN: Broadman &Holman Publishers, 2006), 415.

11: R. Denis Cole, "Numbers," *The New American Commentary*, vol. 3B (Nashville, TN: Broadman &Holman Publishers, 2000), 187.

12: R. Denis Cole, "Numbers," *The New American Commentary*, vol. 3B (Nashville, TN: Broadman &Holman Publishers, 2000), 188-189.

13: Douglas K. Stuart, "Exodus" *The New American Commentary*, vol. 2v (Nashville, TN: Broadman &Holman Publishers, 2006), 417.

14: Ronald E. Clements, "Exodus" *The Cambridge Bible Commentary* (London, UK: Cambridge University Press, 1972), 109.

15: Walter A. Elwell, *Evangelical Dictionary of Theology*, 2nd ed. (Grand Rapids, MI: Baker Academic, 2001), 235.

16: Craig L. Blomberg, "Matthew" *The New American Commentary*, vol. 22 (Nashville, TN: Broadman &Holman Publishers, 1992), 429.

17: R. T. France, "The Gospel of Matthew," *The New International Commentary on the New Testament* (Grand Rapids, MI: William B. Eerdmans Publishing Company, 2007), 1107–1108.

18: R. T. France, "The Gospel of Matthew," *The New International Commentary on the New Testament* (Grand Rapids, MI: William B. Eerdmans Publishing Company, 2007), 1109–1110.

19: Clinton E. Arnold, "Matthew, Mark, Luke," *Zondervan Illustrated Bible Backgrounds Commentary*, vol. 1 (Grand Rapids, MI: Zondervan, 2002), 189.

20: Craig L. Blomberg, "Matthew," *The New American Commentary*, vol. 22 (Nashville, TN: Broadman &Holman Publishers, 1992), 431.

21: Craig L. Blomberg, "Matthew," *The New American Commentary*, vol. 22 (Nashville, TN: Broadman &Holman Publishers, 1992), 433.

CHAPTER TWO

HISTORICAL FOUNDATION OF DISCIPLESHIP

Throughout the ages, history has played a critical role in the lives of individuals. In fact, Christians are people who live with the stuff of church history. History is generally defined as the study of past events, particularly, in human affairs. It is probably in this context that an author wrote that those who cannot learn from history are doomed to repeat it. The 16th century German reformer Philip Melanchthon makes it even clearer: "Human life without knowledge of history is nothing other than a perpetual childhood, nay, a permanent obscurity, and darkness."[1]

The church as an institution makes no exception in chronologically keeping its events. The following statement made by Smither gives a clear understanding of this viewpoint: "In the early church there was a great deal of interest in the lives of the martyrs, saints, monks, and bishops and their memories were preserved through the genre of *hagiography* or through sermons. Church fathers like Augustine and Jerome not only contributed to this body of church literature but encouraged its reading as a means of teaching in the church. Not surprisingly, the authors of hagiography were typically clergy and the audience was generally understood to be the communion of saints."[2]

In light of the church's mission and function to teach the community of faith, Heffernan regards "Hagiography as narratives or literary mosaics that actually served as catechetical tools. Comparing them to the Bible stories housed in the stained glass of medieval cathedrals, he concludes that the primary social function of sacred biography is to teach *(docere)* the truth of the faith through the principle of individual example."[3]

This chapter has explored the ways the church has dealt with its new converts in the past, not only to retain them, but also to help them become disciples. Considering the historical development of the concept of discipleship in the light of this document was very critical. The survey has been very selective because the scope of this endeavor does not necessitate an exhaustive analysis throughout all the past ages. Thus, only some periods have been quickly examined.

First and Second Century

The description of Peter's preaching found in Acts 2:42-47 depicts one of the most plausible discipleship models found in the early Church. The practices outlined in this passage include evangelism, teaching, fellowship, ministry, and worship. Unfortunately, the discipleship model described in this passage did not last long. As Peter, Paul, and most of the other apostles and lay leaders of the first generation of Christians were gone, the Church faced a crisis of leadership. Many of the challenges that the church had encountered could be even traced during the time of the last surviving apostle. Indeed, in the second and fourth chapters of his first epistle, the apostle John gave serious warnings about several antichrists and false teachers, respectively. There is no doubt that the period posed of number of concerns for the Christian church to maintain unity and continue the early discipleship program initiated and found in the book of Acts right after the Pentecost. It is not plausible to give a detailed description of all the problems; however, it appears evident that they were endemic to the growth of the church among the hostile Jewish-Roman world.

However, the vacuum left by the death of the apostles did not remain empty for long. The Church was not passive to this situation. They were understandably concerned with keeping the members and new converts in particular. Explaining the concerns of the early church leaders, Mark Elleingsen shed light on their efforts to disciple their members: "Being alert of these challenges, the Apostolic Fathers developed corpus of writings that would provide the church with a sense of continuity in its beliefs, practices, and polity. There is even some possibility that in the city of Rome a baptismal creed was developed as early as the mid-second century to refute Gnosticism; the formulation eventually evolved into our contemporary versions of the Nicene Creed and the Apostles' Creed."[4]

The Didache: A Discipleship Tool

It is true from a biblical stance that Paul, Peter, and John had addressed the issue of false teachings. However, most heresies widely invaded the church about 300 years after Christ. Therefore, it appears difficult to imagine a first-second century church without solid biblical teachings. The admonition given by the apostle Paul to his young mentee Timothy depicts the importance granted to the Word of God during this era: "But you must continue in the things which you have learned and been assured of, knowing from whom you have learned them, and that from childhood you have known the Holy Scriptures, which are able to make you wise for salvation through faith which is in Christ Jesus. All Scripture is given by inspiration of God, and is profitable for doctrine, for reproof, for correction, for instruction in righteousness, that the man of God may be complete, thoroughly equipped for every good work (2 Ti 3: 14-17)".

Discipleship was mostly presented in a literary form in these epochs. One of the earliest documents written to convey a discipleship endeavor was the Didache. Elleingsen, in his manual, provides good insight about the use of this document as a discipleship tool: "The document clearly embodies very legalistic strictures on how to live, asserting that one either lives according to the way of life or the way of death. Preoccupation with lifestyle standards is evident as the Didache urges the practice of Christian virtues like abstinence, shunning idolatry, patience, humility, and goodness."[5]

The Didache refers to the Teaching of the twelve apostles of Jesus Christ. Some ancient writers even stated that the apostles got this manual (Didache) from the Lord Himself and that they were simply intermediaries. Even though there is no specific proof that the Didache was not written by any of the first century apostles, it remains as one of the most valuable ancient documents that puts emphasis on a discipleship model. Its composite nature contains a lot of excerpts taken from the Gospels, mainly Matthew and Luke, and the epistle of Hebrews. Despite of its small size, the document provided the users with helpful Christian moral standings, and proposed good counsel to the new believers as how to seek and attain spiritual growth.

Since discipleship is the heart of teaching or transmitting the biblical and theological principles of the faith, there is no doubt that the Didache which means teaching has played a significant role in the discipleship process of the early Church. The value of the Didache for the Christian faith resides in the fact that it stresses the role of teaching in the church. The Didache is mentioned to show how the document through its teachings displayed some characteristics of a discipleship model. Therefore, as it is clearly alluded in the Old Testament and emphatically promoted and commanded by Christ in the New Testament, discipleship has always been manifest in the life of the church.

Considering the main components of a discipleship model such as evangelism, teaching, worship, and fellowship, it is plausible to mention that the Didache was an instrumental document about discipleship. Indeed, this idea is greatly supported by the following statement: "The contents may be divided into four parts, which most scholars agree were combined from separate sources by a later redactor. The first is the *Two Ways*, the Way of Life and the Way of Death (chapters 1-6). The second part is a ritual dealing with baptism, fasting, and communion (chs. 7-10). The third speaks of the ministry and how to deal with traveling prophets (chs. 11-15). And the final section (chapter 16) is a brief apocalypse."[6]

With unambiguous and explicit directives given to the members relating to their behavior and the way they should treat one another, these four subdivisions without enigma display the characteristics or the foundation of a discipleship model. Clear and unequivocal instructions are given to the members concerning the way they should treat one another. The document encourages brotherly gatherings among the believers so they could study the Scriptures together, fellowship with one another, and share their problems with each other. That was the best way for them to practice accountability and mutual exhortation as well. A thorough reading of this document will allow discovering most of the Christian ethical principles, such as the Golden Rule (Mt 7: 12), that Jesus taught in the Sermon on the Mount. To become more convinced of a clearer picture of a discipleship program in action during the period understudy, you are advised and invited to carefully read the first letter of Clement, the Didache, and the letter of Ignatius.

Fourteenth through Sixteenth Centuries

Viewed as the state of being a disciple, discipleship during the fourteenth century has been depicted in the person and through the works of John Wycliffe.

His writings laid the preparatory works leading to the Reformation. He put great emphasis on the teachings of the Scriptures. The doctrines, which had been taught by Wycliffe, continued for a time to spread. His followers or disciples were known as Wycliffites and Lollards. They carried the knowledge of the gospel throughout England, and to many other lands. It was through the writings of Wycliffe that John Huss, of Bohemia, was led to renounce many of the errors of Romanism and to enter upon the work of reform. Later the Anabaptists consider discipleship as normative for the Christian life. As for them, believers are to care for one another, and engage in mission to assist non-believers. Discipleship has always been a distinctive mark of God's church.

As mentioned in the introduction, there is no great need to make a thorough study of the discipleship concept throughout all the centuries. However, it is crucial to mention that this concept has always been present in the history of the church. For example, Mark Elleingsen helps to elucidate this viewpoint as he writes, "Samuel Wesley, the son of a Puritan clergyman, was a converted High Church Anglican but clearly a reformer with strategies of renewal much like that of the Pietists. He instituted small-group Bible studies in his parish during John's childhood. The father's influence on his fifteenth child seems evident not just in John's mature orientation towards small Christian nurture but also in his stubborn loyalty to the Church of England as well as its liturgy and polity."[7]

Eighteenth Century, John Wesley and Beyond

Even though it could be felt and even seen in the church life, one needs to admit that discipleship was *timidly* expressed at times. It was not until the eighteenth century that this concept reached a broader significance. This is characterized in the person and the works of John Wesley. Due to his tremendous contribution to church growth and renewal, some time has been put aside to consider the discipleship model that John Wesley put in place in the 18th century.

From the beginning of his career, John Wesley displayed a *convinced* discipleship view. In his book, *Making Disciples*, Matthaei unequivocally expressed this idea while writing, "He understood very early that it is not in making converts but disciples that the church can fulfill the Great Commission. He clearly understood that making disciples is an important ministry of any Christian community."[8] He created three strands of discipleship: societies, classes, and bands so he could implement his discipleship model. In so doing, he really wanted to walk in Jesus' footprints. John's commitment to God and his leadership were unquestionable. Ayling points out his leadership skill and devotion for spiritual matters at the inception of the Holy Club as he writes, "He was not physically present when the Holy Club was founded. However, John had been a mentor at a distance. When he returned to Oxford in November 1729 it was natural that he should take over the leadership."[9] As Wesley took the lead of the Holy club founded by his brother Charles, it was remarkable that discipline had played a critical part in the success of John Wesley's discipleship model.

John Wesley displayed discipleship awareness in the life of new converts. Right after conversion, most Wesleyan theologians state that John showed great interest in transitioning new members to disciples. The key reason was that he wanted them to develop a stable relationship with God and grow spiritually. According to Wesley, the best way for the new believers to attain this goal was to assimilate them into the Christian fellowship through a discipleship program. He did not wait for long to initiate the process. Upon accepting Jesus as their Personal Savior, new converts were encouraged to become members of a special group under the tutoring of an experienced mentor, studying together, praying for one another, and watching over each other. John Wesley was intentional in transforming the new believers from members to disciples.

The particular attention that Wesley brought to new converts had a theological aspect rooted in the Bible. In this case, it makes reasonable sense to go along with Bryant who clearly depicts Wesley's biblical understanding of making disciples. "Wesley understood this discipling process so perceptibly in the light of the scripture that his class structure was permeated with its insights. Aside from the veracity of Scriptures, the experience with the Moravians reinforced Wesley's beliefs in the theological ideal of building up the body of Christ."[10] The necessity of this spiritual progression among new converts can be traced in most of Wesley's sermons but in particular in that on the new birth. He wants the new convert to have a new understanding of life by rejecting the old things and embracing the ones in harmony with the new decisions, they had made. This idea is allegorically expressed in his sermon as he made use of an unborn and a born child. This sermon shows the different steps the new convert should follow to become a mature Christian. This becomes possible through a discipleship process as the new convert remains in church to get the needed instructions. Sugden clearly displays this Wesleyan maturity view of discipleship in the following statement:

"Before a child is born into the world he/she has eyes, but sees not; he/she has ears, but does not hear. He/she has a very imperfect use of any other sense. He/she has no knowledge of any of the things of the world, or any natural understanding. To that manner of existence which he/she then has, we do not even . . . the name of life. It is only when a person, a human being, is born, that life begins. At birth, this living being sees light and gradually the various objects encompassing the new environment come into focus, so different than from inside the womb. Eyes are open and ears able to hear the sounds successively striking them . . . . It is the same situation for a person who has no true knowledge of the things of God, either of spiritual or eternal things. But as soon as that individual is born of God, there is a total change in all these particulars."[11]

One of the key elements of discipleship is fellowship. To make it practical, Wesley intentionally created two special small groups: class meetings and band meetings. The former was required of all members, whereas the latter was optional. The goal was not only to facilitate fellowship, but also to assist each other in their spiritual journey toward holiness. It is widely accepted among the Wesleyan historians that these two groups were the cornerstone of John Wesley's discipleship model.

Class meetings and band meetings were also to promote the spiritual and social development of new converts. They were so vital in early Methodism that they need to be explored much deeper. They formed the basis of the discipleship mentoring model put in place by John Wesley. They were also a means of sharing the Christian experience with those who did not know about God. Although an exhaustive study is not done, this segment will put more emphasis on class meetings, which was critical in making disciples.

The key element of a discipleship model in the class meetings is found in the selection of a leader. A class leader provided oversight. Enumerating the duty of class leaders, Bryant writes: "Each person was responsible for eleven other people. Class leaders recruited and kept attendance for the traveling preacher to review. The leaders were responsible to both the members and preacher. Wesley met once a quarter with every class on every circuit. The class meeting met on a weekly basis and structures were designed for those meetings. Those structures involved the participation and accountability of each person, member, and non-member. They were responsible for class attendance, lesson review, personal accountability, and evangelism."[12]

Class meetings played a critical role in the stability of the Methodist Church in the eighteenth century in the United States. For instance, Linda Bloom, in her article dated November 1, 2004 citing Hardt, not only précised the origination of the class meetings but also showed their stable role in Methodism in New York. "Class meetings originated with John Wesley, the founder of Methodism, in England. The practice continued when Francis Asbury and other circuit-riding preachers brought Methodism to New York from 1766 to 1780. The class system stabilized New York Methodism by developing local church leadership and by monitoring behavior."[13]

Nowadays, millions of people join the church. However, they are not really engaged in the church's activities. They are not involved in any kind of ministry. They do not even know each other's names. There is no Christian bond that links them together. They do not study nor pray together. This is why they become so vulnerable. As one looks back to the experiences of the Christians in the 18th century, it is possible to revive this Christian fellowship. They have faced trials and tribulations, but because they were bound together they have overcome. As we are nearing the Second Coming of Jesus, church members need to be united to support one another. Difficult times are ahead of us; those who sincerely serve the Lord will be persecuted. Let us be united like the disciples, praying to God for the empowering of the Holy Spirit (see Ac 4:23-31). Today's church should revive the practices that kept 18th Century Christians together: small groups with testimony and profound communion, formal Bible study, systematic prayers, and brotherly accountability. All these elements were present in the Wesleyan tradition. They are still relevant to the 21st Century church and constitute the best way to cultivate a living faith in God.

The primary objective of the church today as understood by John Wesley and outlined by Jesus is to make disciples who will become disciple-makers themselves. However, one must confess that there will be no disciples without training. Therefore, it is imperative that the church teach its members how to have a good relationship with God and how they can spread the good news. Good training automatically implies accountability. This liability can be found in John Wesley's Rules for the Band-Societies drawn up on December 25, 1738. In addition to these rules were added some basic questions to those who want to join the bands. Matthaei expresses it this way in her book:

> "The rules for the band were very strict, with eleven questions to be answered upon entering the band and five questions addressed at each meeting:
>
> What known sins have you committed since our last meeting?
> What temptations have you met with?
> How were you delivered?
> What have you thought, said, or done, of which you doubt whether it be sin or not?
> Have you nothing you desire to keep secret?"[14]

Even though they were severe, these Rules were designed for the purpose of maintaining a high level of spirituality among the Christians. They were given for a holy living that can help the disciples grow in a constant relationship with God and their neighbors. The goal of the Rules was beautifully expressed by Matthaei as she wrote. "The Rules for the adult groups in the Methodist movement were intended to provide guidance on the Way of Salvation. They were read frequently in the meetings. And, because of the public nature of the Rules, people knew what was expected of them when they joined the Methodists."[15]

Conclusion

Despite its undeniable apparent success, the Wesleyan discipleship model was not perfect. However, there is no way one can or should undermine the importance of a discipleship program in the church today. History teaches that the spiritual revival that moved England in the middle of the 18th century had its origin in the small-group discipleship model. It is probably in this context that Hardt proposes in his conversation with Linda Bloom the revival of class meetings. She reports, "Hardt believes the revival of class meetings on the local, district or conference levels could benefit current members hungering for more spirituality and prospective members wanting a better grounding in the Christian faith. She goes on saying that will bring a tighter connection among the members. The more intimate setting of the class meeting also provides an opportunity for closer relationships to form and allows members to agree to disagree. By praying together and talking about personal experiences, one tends to bond to these people."[16]

In our modern times, it is impossible to reproduce the Wesleyan discipleship model as it was and expect the same results. The church needs to make all necessary adjustments while they put in place a Christ-based discipleship model for new converts. There were discrepancies in Wesley's, but, since it was Christ-centered, it has successfully worked. When Jesus' followers realize that discipleship is the heart of the Great Commission, plans will be made so discipleship can be at the forefront of all the activities of the church. Even though an exhaustive historical study was not done on discipleship, the few considerations made and the few cases cited allow the conclusion that history has never been silent on that important biblical teaching. Based on what we have learned from the past, there is hope that today's church can be successful in developing and implementing a Christ-based discipleship program for new converts. It therefore requires the desire for holy living. It requires accountability and discipline, the key to this level of holy living. It requires intentionality, participation, and involvement of several entities such as family, school, and church.

1: Gordon L. Heath, *Doing Church History, A User-friendly Introduction to Researching the History of Christianity* (Toronto, Canada: Clements Publishing, 2008), 19.

2: Edward L. Smither, "To Emulate and Imitate, Possidus' Life of Augustine as a Fifth Century Discipleship Tool," *Southwestern Journal of Theology*, March 1, 2008: 1.

3: Edward L. Smither, "To Emulate and Imitate, Possidus' Life of Augustine as a Fifth Century Discipleship Tool," *Southwestern Journal of Theology*, March 1, 2008: 1.

4: Mark Elleingsen, *Reclaiming Our Roots, An Inclusive Introduction to Church History*, vol. 1 (Harrisburg, PA: Trinity Press International,

1999), 61.

5: Mark Elleingsen, *Reclaiming Our Roots, An Inclusive Introduction to Church History*, vol. 1 (Harrisburg, PA: Trinity Press International, 1999), 37, 38.

6: Didache, accessed June 4, 2014, http://en.wikipedia.org/wiki/Didache.

7: Mark Elleingsen, *Reclaiming Our Roots, An Inclusive Introduction to Church History*, vol. 2 (Harrisburg, PA: Trinity Press International, 1999), 183, 184.

8: Sondra Higgins Matthaei, *Making Disciples, Faith Formation In the Wesleyan Tradition*, (Nashville, TN: Abingdon Press, 2000), 17.

9: Stanley Ayling, *John Wesley*, (Cleveland. New York: William Collins Publishers, Inc., 1979), 45

10: Donald Earl Bryant Sr., *Retaining and Engaging Members In The Life Of The Congregation*, (D.Min Thesis, United Theological Seminary in Trotwood, OH, June 2007), 44, 45.

11: Edward H. Sugden, *John Wesley's Fifty-three Sermons* (Nashville: Abingdon Press, 1983), 571, 572

12: Donald Earl Bryant Sr., *Retaining and Engaging Members In The Life Of The Congregation* (D.Min Thesis, United Theological Seminary in Trotwood, OH, June 2007), 45, 46.

13: Linda Bloom: Class Meetings, a part of Methodist History, have Relevance Today (http://archives.umc.org/interior.asp?ptid=2&mid=5937, November 1, 2004), accessed October 8, 2012

14: Sondra Higgins Matthaei: Making Disciples, Faith Formation In the Wesleyan Tradition (Nashville, TN: Abingdon Press, 2000), 55.

15: Sondra Higgins Matthaei: Making Disciples, Faith Formation In the Wesleyan Tradition (Nashville, TN: Abingdon Press, 2000), 135.

16: Linda Bloom: Class Meetings, a part of Methodist History, have Relevance Today (http://archives.umc.org/interior.asp?ptid =2&mid=5937, November 1, 2004), accessed October 8, 2012

CHAPTER THREE

THEOLOGICAL FOUNDATION OF DISCIPLESHIP

To be viable, a discipleship program for new converts should have a theological grounding, which depicts a clear understanding of salvation and the implications of its components in the life of the new convert. This chapter presents two main theological themes, soteriology and ecclesiology. Though there has not been an exhaustive study of these two terms, they set the theological foundation of this discipleship program. The purpose is simply to show the importance of their interrelation, and how the new convert can prepare to inherit eternal life at Jesus' return even as they disciple others. The theological works of John Wesley on Salvation and those of a few others on Church have been considered in the light of this endeavor.

Soteriology and Ecclesiology

The sole purpose of accepting Jesus as Lord and Savior is to have everlasting salvation. However, as we consider Jesus' teaching regarding salvation, it is easily understood that salvation is not a one-time or a point action. It is clearly stated in the Word of God that the one who perseveres until the end shall have eternal life (Mt 24: 13). Thus, the thought, "once saved always saved," is not biblical and has no theological ground. As per this consideration, there is no doubt that soteriology plays a critical role in the lives of those who call themselves Christians, particularly in the lives of new converts. In other words, to be a disciple, the new convert needs to know and understand the scope of the decision to walk with Jesus. It is interesting to note that the place or location designed or chosen by Christ for the on-going teaching of this critical biblical doctrine is none other than the church.

John Wesley as Theologian

In the beginning, John Wesley was mostly seen as the founder of Methodism rather than a theologian. Some theologians and scholars have found it easy to dismiss him and this title. It was perhaps in this context that Borgen has written "For many years, John Wesley was given a rather romantic image as Father of Methodism and the man with the warm heart while his theology was largely ignored... Today his position as a theologian is generally recognized."[1] John Wesley might not be a systematic theologian. However, when we consider Wesley's emphasis on salvation and many other theological components, one can say without ambiguity that he has developed a practical theology structured around the *Ordo Salutis*, which is God's work in redeeming man. There-fore, there is no doubt that John Wesley was a theologian.

Wesley and Salvation

The Wesleyan theology grants a great importance to salvation. In other words, John Wesley presents salvation as the entire redeeming work of God in the life of an individual. He considers salvation as the end of the Christian religion, and the means to obtain it is faith through a life of holiness. Borgen writing about Wesley's theology states,

"Wesley builds all his principles and doctrines on Scripture and common sense. Consequently, according to the analogy of faith and the grand scheme of doctrines in the Scriptures, he subscribes to the three grand, essential, and fundamental scriptural doctrines of original sin, justification by faith, and sanc-tification translated as inward and outward holiness. These are the central doc-trines in Wesley's theology."[2]

The development of a Christ-based discipleship model for new converts needs to convey a clear teaching about salvation. In the *Handbook of Seventh-day Adventist Theology*, Ivan T. Blazen helps understand the global aspect of salvation. "Salvation is the universal theme of Scripture. All other major themes are subdivisions or explications of it. The form of salvation varies, but the underlying structure is the same: God visits his people and delivers them from problems or powers that imperil their existence."[3]

Salvation is a critical biblical teaching. It is therefore extremely important that new converts know what it entails. This might be one of the main reasons that it occupies a crucial role in the writings of John Wesley. To help catch Wesley's theological emphasis on salvation, Borgen states,

"These truths are brought to light by the gospels. Whether it is said that these two heads of doctrine include the essential doctrines of original sin, justification by faith and sanctification; or, as Wesley says another place: Our main doctrines, which include all the rest, are three—that of Repentance, of Faith, and Holiness – matters not so much for Wesley. When he speaks of God or any person within the Godhead, it is always seen in relation to God's love and redemption of man; and when he speaks of the way of salvation it is always seen in the context of the atonement and the ongoing work of salvation through the Holy Spirit. Consequently, these doctrines form the essential core of Wesley's theology and, as such, can properly be deemed fundamental."[4]

As long as they are in this carnal body and live in this corrupt and sinful environment, God's people will have the need for divine salvation. Because sin creates separation between us and God (Is 59: 2), new converts have to acknowledge their powerlessness and claim the help of God to overcome the dominating power of sin. Salvation is thus an act of God's grace through the death of Jesus Christ for us on the cross of Calvary. New converts need a new heart and right spirit. The renewal of the heart plays a crucial role in Wesley's theology. Gregory Clapper notes that "Wesley's emphasis on the affections and the heart makes a strong case for seeing the renewing of the heart was the most essential element of Wesley's vision of Christianity. In his sermon on Original Sin, Wesley says that the great end of religion is to renew our hearts in the image of God."[5]

New converts have been taught of the importance of repentance, forgiveness, renewal, and sanctification in order to live the new heart experience. Clapper making echo of *Albert Outler's* comment on the renewing of the heart writes that "the renewal of the heart is the axial theme of Wesley's soteriology. Almost every thinker who has studied Wesley agrees that soteriology is at the center of his theology."[6] Living in a world devastated by sin and dominated by evil powers, new converts need to know the provisions made for them through the plan of salvation. The solution of sin lies in a new relationship with God, a new assurance before God, and a new life from God.

Salvation has diverse components: justification and righteousness, reconciliation, adoption, repentance and conversion, sanctification, and so many more. To help new converts grasp the meaning of this biblical doctrine, emphasis has been put on justification and sanctification. Indeed, John Wesley, in his soteriology puts great accent on these two components with faith as the common denominator. In general, right after baptism, new converts face many challenges. As per instructions received during evangelistic series, they want to live a sinless life and make every effort to accomplish this, but it is always impossible. The biggest problem is that they try to make it on their own. Special teachings on salvation have been given to help new converts not to be fearful but rather to count on Jesus' merits to fight and overcome evil.

Justification

New converts have been not only instructed as to the importance of justification, but also are taught that justification is a gift of God. All that is needed is to be accepted by faith. Justification was completed on the cross. It is not something for them to complete. Once new converts have a clear theological view of the doctrine of justification, they will be more determined to continue the spiritual journey, regardless of the constant appearance of sin in their lives. Commenting on Wesley's teaching of justification, Oden states, "The plain scriptural notion of justification is pardon, forgiveness of sins. It is that act of God the Father whereby, for the sake of the propitiation made by the blood of his Son, he shows forth his righteousness by the remission of the sins that are past. To those justified by faith, God will not impute sin to his condemnation."[7] How encouraging it is for new converts to know that all of their past sins in thought, word, and deed are covered and blotted out and shall not be remembered or mentioned against them any longer? This idea is well-expressed by the apostle Paul in his second letter to the Christians of Corinth, "Therefore, if anyone is in Christ, he is a new creation; old things have passed away; behold, all things have become new" (2 Co 5: 17). Justification is thus a forensic declaration, a verdict credited in our favor, God's act for us.

Sanctification

Sanctification can be viewed as a daily and continuous work toward salvation. Oden defines it as the second component of Wesley's teaching of salvation, which he encourages all his associates to teach with intentionality. "The second part of John Wesley's more limited sense of salvation is called sanctification. Justification is what God does for us through his Son. Sanctification is what God works in us by his Spirit. It is the immediate fruit of justification. Wesley equates sanctification to holiness. John Wesley urged that all preachers in his connection of spiritual formation make a point of teaching the way of holiness to believers constantly, strongly and explicitly, and that all class leaders should be attentive to this doctrine and continually agonize for its experiential appropriation".[8]

Writing on this biblical doctrine, Blazen states, "Sanctification, or holiness, is one of the most frequent, important, and all-embracing concepts in Scripture. It has to do with God and man; with relationships, worship, and morals; with every period of life, whether past, present, or future; and with every element of the world, including times and places, objects and rituals. It is so significant that believers are admonished to strive for holiness without which no one will see the Lord (Heb.12:14)."[9]

Through sound biblical teaching of sanctification, new converts must realize that they are set apart for God. They cannot be of the world any longer. They cannot eat the same way they used to. They cannot go some places they used to. At this level, new converts are to seek for holiness as it is written in Leviticus 19:2: You shall be holy; for I the Lord your God am holy. Sanctification becomes avail and possible to new converts by virtue of their new relationship with God. Holiness produces a union between the believer and Christ. As they become united to Christ, new converts should not let sin reign in their mortal bodies; rather, they should yield their members to God as weapons of righteousness.

On John Wesley's *Scriptural Christianity*, Oden presents Wesley's teaching of sanctification. He writes, according to John Wesley, that "By sanctification one was saved from sin's power and root and restored to God's image. Sanctification had as its outcome, even in this life, the perfection of the believer, entire sanctification. For Wesley, perfection was not a static, but a dynamic reality, not a perfected perfection but a perfecting perfection. Wesley saw perfection as overcoming pride, self-will, evil tempers and thoughts, and restoring the mind of Christ. For him, entire sanctification was love excluding sin; love filling the heart, taking up the whole capacity of the soul."[10] This Christ-based discipleship model has clearly stated for new converts that sanctification is a constant movement forward. It is a continuous action for the Christian. In other words, sanctification for the new believer is a journey without end. There may be fulfillment, but not finality; further advances are always to be made.

Ecclesiology

Jesus makes no more mention of an explicit ecclesiology than does the Old Testament. However, when we study the structure of the early church, we discover that the church was seen as a loving and sharing family (Acts 4:32). That makes us understand that the converts were not an isolated group of people but rather a community of believers devoted in serving the Lord. Upon accepting Jesus as personal Savior and becoming His disciples, new converts are required to live up the principles or standards set by Christ. They must practice love and show the willingness to sacrifice themselves. In following the ideal model of the early Christian church found in the book of Acts, the neophytes will not only value the church but also will remain in this new community of faith to further their knowledge and perfect their relationships with Jesus. Luke, in Acts 2: 42, encourages the new believers to attend the teachings of the church, participate in the breaking of the bread, involve in corporate worship and prayer, and practice deeds of charitable nature.

Despite Christ's radical statement about His church (see Mt 16:18), several people continue to undermine its importance. New converts need to know much more about the church. In fact, when He was on earth, Jesus was not a lone ranger. Ronald J. Sider gives a good description of the church that he views as the visibility of God's kingdom. "Christ did not travel around the countryside declaring God's forgiveness to isolated hermits. Jesus formed a new society. He gathered a new community of forgiven disciples, who challenged evil and proclaimed the gospel."[11] This viewpoint has been reinforced by Bell when he writes, "Jesus ministered with a community of close disciples, and He transformed them from a raw band of individuals into a Christian mission community that would expand the boundaries of Israel beyond its national identity (John 17:11)."[12] New converts need to know that upon their acceptance of Jesus they become part of a God-established community. Indeed, the

Godhead has always worked as a team (Gn 1:26; 2:22; 11:7; Is 6:8, etc.). Christ has built and valued His church. On His encounter with Saul on the road of Damascus, Jesus could have told him all he needed to know in order to begin his ministry. However, He rather sent Saul, later Paul, to a church leader, Ananias, to give him further instructions about his apostleship. I strongly believe that angels are smarter than human beings. The angel that was sent to Cornelius could have also taught him more about God. But the Lord had him send for Peter, a church official, to explain to him the Word of God.

The church is a divine institution established by Christ for the welfare of humankind. Christ was intentional when he laid the foundation of the New Testament church. From the foremost, Christ began to gather to Himself a number of disciples, and also gave them memorable teachings about the manner of life they were meant to live. Church and salvation are intertwined to bring human salvation to its completeness. In other words, the church is God's appointed agency for the salvation of sinners. If you biblically think that some change needs to be done, you must stay in the church to promote it. For, as good as a soccer player is, he cannot score for his team if he is outside the field game. Therefore, new converts should understand shortly after conversions that leaving the church is not always a good decision to make.

Some Theologians and the Church

The church may not be always what God wants it to be, but it is precious to Him. As God's children, we are to value His house as well. The reverent attitude toward this institution was clearly manifested in the life of King David when he wrote, "I was glad when they said unto me, Let us go into the house of the LORD (Ps 122: 1)." The psalmist Asaph seemed to suggest the same direction to take when we are facing trials and unsolved problems (see Ps 73). Therefore, regardless of the limits and weaknesses, new convert must acknowledge the existence and importance of the church. The view of the church as God's agency on earth is reinforced by Ellen G. White as she writes, "The church of Christ, enfeebled and defective as it may be, is the only object on earth on which He bestows His supreme regard. The Lord has a people, a chosen people, His church, to be His own, His own fortress, which He holds in a sin-stricken, revolted world."[13]

New converts generally come from different religious backgrounds that at times undermine the importance of the church. Several people said that they do not need the church. All they need is a good relationship with God, which they can find in their own homes. Thus, it leaves no doubt that doing ecclesiology in this context is not something easy. Not only does Vickers point out the problem but he also proposes a solution: "Among our growing anxiety about the church, we ought to be doing ecclesiology on our knees. Far from shouting at one another, we need to enter into a round of prayerful reflection on what the church is called by God to be and to do in the world. The proper way to begin this prayerful reflection is not by naming what is wrong with the church or by making a case for how to put things right, and we certainly shouldn't begin by deciding who is to blame. Rather, we should begin by reflecting prayerfully on what sort of community the church is."[14]

Most challenges encountered inside or outside the church today are caused by the fact that people are ignorant about the scope of the church. Some come to church with the assumption that all their needs will be met while they overlook the responsibilities that becoming part of the church brings. To help new converts get a summing up idea of the church, this section has put accent on the nature and mission of the church.

Nature of the Church
The church is built on Christ and founded on what has been accomplished through Christ. However, a church without the presence of the Holy Spirit is a dead and worthless church. Therefore, Christology and pneumatology must be seen as the two critical elements to describe the nature of the church. Without Christ the church can do nothing; and without the empowering of the Holy Spirit, the church cannot fulfill its mission (Mt 28:20; Ac 1:8).

At their very entrance, new converts should have in mind a clear vision of the nature of the church. To elucidate this point, Vickers rightly writes, "Understanding the nature of the church in light of the church's Pentecostal origins enables us truly to attribute holiness, unity, catholicity, and apostolicity to the church. Similarly, it enables us rightly to attribute to the church the exemplary qualities suggested by the New Testament metaphors for the church."[15] Jesus began his ministry, saying that the kingdom of God is at hand (Mk 1:15). Being Christ's ambassador on earth, the church has the same function. Contrasting the Kingdom of God with the church, Raoul Dederen states that "the church is the human community that lives under God's rule. Created in answer to the call of the gospel of the kingdom, the church witnesses to the kingdom. The kingdom is God's redeeming activity in Christ in the world; the church is the assembly of those called out of the world, who are redeemed and belong to Christ. The church is the manifestation of the kingdom or reign of God."[16] A good comprehension of the nature of the church will help the new converts to remain steadfast and get them ready to know and embrace the mission of the church.

Mission of the Church

As the body of Christ, the church has not been called to exist as an end plan, but rather as a fulfillment of God's purpose. It has to carry on the Lord's ministry in the world, to do what Jesus would do if He were still on earth. In addition to sharing the gospel message with the unsaved, baptizing those who believe in Christ, teaching and nurturing its members, the main purpose of the church is to glorify God (1Cor 10:31; Eph 3:10). Vickers summarizes all these functions of the church in a twofold mission of the church. "The Holy Spirit enables and empowers the church to do two things. On the one hand, the Holy Spirit is ever at work in the church, enabling her to worship God. On the other hand, the Holy Spirit is ever at work in the church, enabling her to bear witness to the life, death, and resurrection of Jesus Christ."[17]

The primary task of the church is to worship God. We are living in a secular world where worship is not really appreciated. Worship should be the first basic element new converts must be aware of in their journey with Jesus. As they worship the Creator, they bring glory to God, listen to the proclamation of the Word, and participate in the sacraments. It is in the context of the church that the new believer experiences true and corporate worship. New converts are called to cultivate authentic relationships with other believers through fellowships and worship. In other terms, corporate worship is a necessity for new converts to grow horizontally and vertically.

Another key task of the church consists of making disciples. This is the final commission Jesus gave to His disciples before ascending to heaven. This constitutes the job description of the church and by extension of every member, and of every new convert. Throughout the Bible, God is portrayed as a God of sending of mission. Thus, as they become disciples, new converts have the responsibility to share the good news of Jesus Christ with those with whom they are in contact. Every new convert ought to know that God has chosen to depend on the church to forward his work of salvation. And to enable us to accomplish this task, He promises to pour out the Holy Spirit upon us.

As we study thoroughly Jesus' great commission to the disciples, another mission of the church is expressed unequivocally. This is the mission of teaching. In other words, the edification of the new believers or new converts is another mission of the church. New converts need to grow up in Christ before becoming efficient disciples or witnesses. Teaching must play a vital role in the life of the church if we want to witness effectively. In fact, the instruction of new converts is not something optional but a requirement of Jesus himself. Matthew's account of the Great Commission clearly indicates that it takes more than just preaching to make disciples for the kingdom of God. It requires that we teach them as well.

Conclusion

To become not simply church members but Christ's disciples, new converts need to recognize that God's act enabling us to have eternal life has been made once and for all. However, at the same time they have to understand that salvation is a continuous process of accepting and living in permanent relationship with Jesus. And the church is the center established by God to live this salvific reality. We are not to seek perfection in the church; we are not going to find it. Jesus is our perfect model and example. Before officially starting His earthly ministry, Christ was found Himself in the Temple (church) at the age of 12, discussing with the ecclesial authorities about His Father's affairs (read Lk 2:41-49). It was His custom to regularly attend church's services (Lk 4:16). Let everyone who call themselves Christ's followers imitate or follow His example. Until Christ's Second Coming there will be healthy and sick people in the church. Jesus, in the parable of the tares found in the 13th chapter of the Gospel of Matthew, verses 24-30, instructs us to leave both categories live together. Jesus-Christ is the Great physician. The church is the clinical where He cares for and heals the sick. Stop giving false excuses not to join the Assembly of God due to its deficiencies. The church, His body, represents a city of refuge; it is the voice of God's redemptive plan for sinners on earth. As one considers the nature and mission of the church, it is crucial to invite the broken in and the Holy Spirit will produce the transformative work.

This chapter shows without enigma that discipleship has theological foundation. Jesus, the Initiator of discipleship, is portrayed as the Savior of the human race. Luke makes it plain in the book of Acts, "Nor is there salvation in any other, for there is no other name under heaven given among men by which we must be saved (Ac 4: 12)." That was indeed the mission of Jesus (Lk 19: 10) when He came on this earth. However, when Jesus saves someone, He does not automatically bring them to heaven. The Bible says that he adds them to his church. "And the Lord added to the church daily those who were being saved (Ac 2: 47)." Referring to the church as a new community for new believers, Stott writes: "Peter was not asking for private and individual conversions only, but for a public identification with other believers. Commitment to the Messiah implied commitment to the Messianic community, that is, the church."[18] It is not in Jesus' plan for new converts to abandon the church or to cut themselves off the Body of Christ. Soteriology and ecclesiology are intertwined to get us ready for glorification at Christ's Return.

The new convert needs to be convinced that whoever accepts Christ as their personal Savior stands justified before God and has eternal life. However, they must pursue sanctification through total surrender, prayer, and the study of the Word of God to maintain this salvific relationship with Jesus. While He is getting ready to come again, Christ has built His church upon Himself to prepare His people to meet with Him. Regardless of the attacks of the enemy, Christ's church (Mt 16: 16-18) has been and will be victorious. Salvation is not a dream but a reality in Christ, the Son of God. "And this is the testimony: that God has given us eternal life, and this life is in His Son. He who has the Son has life; he who does not have the Son of God does not have life. These things I have written to you who believe in the name of the Son of God, that you may know that you have eternal life, and that you may continue to believe in the name of the Son of God (1 Jn 5: 11-13)."

1: Ole E. Borgen, *John Wesley on the Sacraments*, (Zurich, Switzerland: Publishing House of the United Methodist Church, 1972), 36.

2: Ole E. Borgen, *John Wesley on the Sacraments*, (Zurich, Switzerland: Publishing House of the United Methodist Church, 1972), 42.

3: Ivan T. Blazen, *Handbook of Seventh-day Adventist Theology*, vol. 12. Edited by George W. Reid, Commentary Reference (Hagerstown, MD: Review and Herald Publishing Association, 2000), 271.

4: Ole E. Borgen, *John Wesley on the Sacraments*, (Zurich, Switzerland: Publishing House of the United Methodist Church, 1972), 43.

5: Gregory S. Clapper, *The Renewal of the Heart Is The Mission Of The Church: Wesley's Heart Religion In The Twenty-First Century*, (Eugene, OR: Cascade Books, 2010), 27.

6: Gregory S. Clapper, *The Renewal of the Heart Is The Mission Of The Church: Wesley's Heart Religion In The Twenty-First Century*, (Eugene, OR: Cascade Books, 2010), 27.

7: Thomas C. Oden, *John Wesley's Scriptural Christianity*, (Grand Rapids, MI: Zondervan Publishing House, 1994), 199.

8: Thomas C. Oden, *John Wesley's Scriptural Christianity* (Grand Rapids, MI: Zondervan Publishing House, 1994), 311.

9: Ivan T. Blazen, *Handbook of Seventh-day Adventist Theology*, vol. 12. Edited by George W. Reid, Commentary Reference (Hagerstown, MD: Review and Herald Publishing Association, 2000), 295.

10: Thomas C. Oden, *John Wesley's Scriptural Christianity*, (Grand Rapids, MI: Zondervan Publishing House, 1994), 306.

11: Ronald, J. Sider, *Good News and Good Works: A Theology of the Whole Gospel* (Grand Rapids, MI: Baker Books, 1983), 57.

12: Skip Bell, editor, *Servants & Friends: A Biblical Theology of Leadership* (Berrien Springs, MI: Andrews University Press, 2014), 380.

13: Ellen G. White, *In Heavenly Places*. (Hagerstown, MD. Review and Herald Publishing Association, 1995), 284.

14: Jason E. Vickers, *Minding the Good Ground: A Theology for Church Renewal* (Waco, TX: Baylor University Press, 2011), 21.

15: Jason E. Vickers, *Minding the Good Ground: A Theology for Church Renewal* (Waco, TX: Baylor University Press, 2011), 36, 37.

16: Raoul Dederen, *Handbook of Seventh-day Adventist Theology*, vol. 12. Edited by George W. Reid, Commentary Reference (Hagerstown, MD: Review and Herald Publishing Association, 2000), 543.

17: Jason E. Vickers, *Minding the Good Ground: A Theology for Church Renewal* (Waco, TX: Baylor University Press, 2011), 53.

18: John R. W. Stott, *The Message of Acts: The Spirit, the Church, and the World* (Downers Grove, IL: Inter-Varsity Press, 1994), 78, 79.

CHAPTER FOUR
EVANGELISM: SEEKING THE LOST

It is impossible to conceive a discipleship program without evangelism. In the ancient world, God placed Israel at the crossroads of the nations so they could make people know about Him. Most scholars argue that there was no specific mandate to do evangelism in the Old Testament times. Debating what some practical theologians or missiologists say or think is not the focus of this chapter. The bottom line is that God has always had an evangelistic plan to reveal Himself to humankind. The Old Testament is filled with plausible cases affirming God's plan of salvation to all. Thus, coming to Israel was not the only way to have knowledge about God. For instance, the prophets of the Lord were not ministering only to His people, but also prophesied about other nations and called them to repentance. God has been concerned with all nations; His sending of Jonah to Nineveh is an irrefutable example. He even sometimes brought His chosen ones to captivity in order to proclaim His goodness to the heathen world. Jesus' command found in Matthew 28: 19 is not really a new directive but a requirement for all believers. The "Go" that introduces the mandate equates "evangelize."This present chapter will discuss the importance and the reasons of doing evangelism. Based on Christ's way of proclaiming the good news, the chapter will also introduce some key biblical and universal principles for a successful evangelism strategy.

Evangelism: Definition

Before we go any further in this chapter, it is important that we understand what evangelism means; in other words, what is evangelism? There is not a singular or specific definition for evangelism. However, in its broadest terms and particularly in the context of making disciples, evangelism may be defined as the process of winning people to Jesus Christ and enabling them to be transformed by God into responsible disciples who are ready to meet Jesus when He comes.[ii] This definition leaves no doubt that evangelism and discipleship are intertwined. When we, God's people, better understand Him and His mission, we will discover that we serve an evangelistic God. God's evangelistic nature is revealed after the fall in Genesis 3:9: "Then the Lord God called to Adam and said to him, 'Where are you?'" God is the One who seeks. The phrase: "Where are you?" is in the background of everything throughout the rest of Scripture. In other terms, the rest of scripture is about the seeking God: through Moses, the prophets, Christ, and the disciples. This viewpoint is well understood through Christ's mission statement inserted in Luke 19:10: "for the Son of Man has come to seek and to save that which was lost."

Since the Bible throughout its pages presents a seeking God, what does this mean for the church today? Being God's representative on earth, the church is called to be involved in God's mission, which is seeking the lost. As God's people and ambassadors, as God's imitators, we must be channels through which God keeps seeking the unsaved, which is the heart of evangelism. Christ died for every single individual; thus, the salvation that He offers must be made available to all. It is our responsibility to tell them about the love of God manifested in Jesus' sacrificial death. The apostle Peter gives convincing insight about our mission after being saved. God's plan is that the church be the people of God for the sake of the nations, those who do not know Him. We are the people of God for the sake of God's seeking heart, "But you are a chosen people, a royal priesthood, a holy nation, God's special possession, that you may declare the praises of him who called you out of darkness into his wonderful light" (1 Pt 2:9). In other words, we are called out of the world and then put back into the world to proclaim the good news of salvation. Thus, evangelism is not an option, but rather a divine requirement for all the called out ones. Our mission is unequivocally defined in the Great Commission: seeking the lost, pointing them to Jesus, and making them disciples.

Christ's Way and Method of doing Evangelism

As one considers attentively Christ's earthly ministry, it is plausible to discover that evangelism is not as complicated as people generally imagine. To be successful in doing evangelism, we need to "make it simple" like Christ did. The gospels clearly show the simple way the Savior evangelized to people. For instance, Matthew reports that He had compassion for them and taught them about the kingdom of God. "Then Jesus went about all the cities and villages, teaching in their synagogues, preaching the gospel of the kingdom, and healing every sickness and every disease among the people. But when He saw the multitudes, He was moved with compassion for them, because they were weary and scattered, like sheep having no shepherd (Mt.9: 35, 36)." These verses pictured the three pillars that constituted Christ's method of evangelism: teaching, preaching, and healing.

To be successful in evangelism, Ellen G. White suggested that we follow Christ's modus operandi as she wrote, "Christ's method alone gives true success in reaching the people. The Savior mingled with men as one who desired their good. He showed his sympathy for them, ministered to their needs, and won their confidence. Then He bade them, "Follow me"."[1] This statement elucidates without any doubt Christ's way of sharing the good news of salvation and later of making disciples. Thus, one does not need to be a Bible teacher, a pastor, or a theologian to do evangelism. Evangelism is simply admitting that you are a sinner, believing in Jesus as your personal Savior, and confessing the name of Jesus Christ to others. In other terms, evangelism is telling other people what Jesus has done for you, and/or how he has changed your life.

The story of the Samaritan woman reported in the Gospel of John displays at least four crucial principles indicating that everybody is capable of doing evangelism. The first principle is that one does not need to know a lot to tell about Jesus. The second principle is that we need not spend a lot of time to tell about Christ. The third principle is that we need not the permission or authorization from anyone to share the good news about Jesus. And the fourth principle we want to mention underlines the simplicity in telling about Jesus Christ. The woman had not been baptized yet. She did not attend and graduate from a theological seminary. After her encounter with Christ, John simply writes, "The woman then left her water pot, went her way into the city, and said to the men, 'Come, see a Man who told me all things that I ever did. Could this be the Christ?' Then they went out of the city and came to Him (John 4: 28-30)." This story presents two great results of personal testimony:

The first, immediate, and short-term result is found in verses 39 through 42, where many Samaritans came to see and listen to Jesus for themselves. "And many of the Samaritans of that city believed in Him because of the word of the woman who testified, 'He told me all that I ever did.' So when the Samaritans had come to Him, they urged Him to stay with them; and He stayed there two days. And many more believed because of His own word. Then they said to the woman, 'Now we believe, not because of what you said, for we ourselves have heard Him and we know that this is indeed the Christ, the Savior of the world.'" (John 4: 39-42)."

The second, mid- or long-term result can be traced in the eighth chapter of the book of Acts. The proclamation of that woman is seen by several scholars as the groundwork of the evangelistic success in Samaria after persecution had broken in Jerusalem against the disciples. "Then Philip went down to the city of Samaria and preached Christ to them. And the multitudes with one accord heeded the things spoken by Philip, hearing and seeing the miracles which he did. But when they believed Philip preaching the things concerning the kingdom of God, and the name of Jesus Christ, they were baptized, both men and women (Acts 8: 5, 6, 12)."

Intentional Evangelism

Transforming new converts from members to Disciples of Christ requires intentional evangelism. Intentional evangelism is a way of life that leads people to the Lordship of Jesus Christ. Doing intentional evangelism is to make our presence (individual and/or congregation) noticed wherever we are through words and deeds. After being acknowledged for doing good to others, we must not only turn the eyes of the beneficiaries to the Savior who makes us capable of acting properly, but also encourage them to initiate and develop their own personal relationship with the Savior. This starting friendship with Jesus will be improved through assimilation in the church's activities and teaching of the Word of God. At this stage, one becomes a mature disciple, who will reproduce the work of the Master, which is to make disciples.

Intentional evangelism can be done through personal and public evangelism. Based on the story of the Samaritan woman, personal evangelism can be perceived as the sharing of the activity of God in one's life. In addition, it involves careful listening to the spiritual needs of others for whom one intercedes regularly. It also means the study of the Word of God with them while requesting the Holy Spirit to bring them conviction of their sins, repentance and acceptance of Jesus as Lord and Savior. The Gospel of John shows how powerful personal evangelism, testimony or witnessing is. From the beginning with John the Baptist to the end with Mary, emphasis has been put on personal evangelism. We would like to testify that personal evangelism still has the same persuasive power for our post-modern society today.

In 1997, I was leading a collegiate Sabbath School class. We regularly visited with people in the community every second Sabbath of the month. One afternoon while entering a building, we saw a lady uneasily carrying several grocery bags. She was very pleased when some of us helped her to carry these bags inside her apartment. After thanking us, she gave us a list of apartments where we could find the ethnic group targeted in our visits. That same day, we met a twenty-three-year-old young lady who agreed to study the Bible with us. Because her house was not convenient, she took us to her parents' apartment. As the study went along, her relatives opposed our coming to their house. We managed to pursue the Bible study, and about five months later she gave her heart to Jesus through baptism. The church did the best to nurture her, and three years later, her mom and dad got baptized as well.

In 2012, we had an evangelistic series in our church. A female member befriended a lady that she had met for the very first time at the laundromat and invited her to the meetings. The same night she honored the invitation. The next day, she brought her entire six-member family. They attended the rest of the series without missing a day, and four of them got baptized at the end of the campaign. The two remaining were children too young to decide. Another woman who attended the meetings, even before accepting Christ, invited four other friends who gave their lives to Jesus as well. These testimonies are given to prove that personal evangelism is still convincing and powerful to bring souls to the Lord.

Public evangelism is done through campaigns, small groups settings, and high-level seminars. Some critics minimize the importance of public evangelism. Some even advance that Jesus did not hold evangelistic series. Those myths about public evangelism are wrong and completely false. The gospels clearly show that Jesus utilized both approaches (private and public). His encounters with Nicodemus and the Samaritan woman, for example, are cases of personal evangelism. However, when he taught, preached to the crowds, he was doing public evangelism. In fact, as a result of public evangelism, the early church grew 26 times in just one day (from 120 to 3,120). The apostle Paul used the Acts 20/20 vision or approach (personal, or private, and public evangelism). The book of Acts is filled with cases of public evangelism.

Christ's command before his ascension was to make disciples. However, it is impossible to make disciples without firstly doing evangelism. Evangelism is not a one-time event. It is rather a lifestyle where public evangelism must be seen for a reaping event. In other terms, evangelism is a process, of which public evangelism is the reaping part. The process consists of sowing or planting through invitation (come and see), cultivating through friendship evangelism, and reaping or harvesting through soul-winning. We just cannot bypass evangelism if we want to fulfill the Great Commission. Evangelism and discipleship are the two main intertwined components of Jesus' final assignment to the disciples and to us per extension.

Ten Biblical Principles for a Successful Evangelistic Series

As for those who think that public evangelism is a waste of money, time, and energy, we want to reiterate that there has not been great dilemma with this means of sharing globally the gospel. The problem may rather be a lack of good preparation. To be successful, any evangelistic endeavor needs and must be well prepared. Winning souls for Christ cannot be the result of chance and negligence. In fact, presenting Christ to the lost is the most important thing in life and the best "merchandise" we can offer to them. Therefore, this must be done with care, passion, and love. Before undermining the importance of public evangelism, take the time to prayerfully read and implement the following ten biblical, universal principles that generally lead to a successful evangelistic series.

Principle #1: Assurance of God's Presence

The first biblical principle of success when conducting an evangelistic endeavor is to have the assurance that God is with us. Having God's direction is all we need. With God's presence, success is assured. It is not a human activity but a cosmic battle (Eph.6:12). Thus, we must do all we can to make sure that Jesus is leading. This principle can be traced in both Old Testament and New Testament. "And the Lord said to Joshua, Have I not commanded you? Be strong and courageous. Do not be afraid; do not be discouraged, for the LORD your God will be with you wherever you go.'" (Jos. 1:9). Jesus on His part tells His disciples, "Apart from me you can do nothing (John 15: 5b)." We can glean a positive attitude from this principle because the One who sends us has all authority in heaven and on earth, and promises to be with us in this endeavor. He makes His Holy Spirit available to us to perform the task as stated by Zechariah. "So he answered and said to me:' This is the word of the LORD to Zerubbabel: Not by might nor by power, but by My Spirit,' says the LORD of hosts (Zec.4:6).'"

Principle #2: Prayer

The second biblical principle that leads to a successful evangelistic series is prayer. The most important activity in preparation for the meetings is to get the church members praying for them. We must always remember that people are not reached by human persuasion and logic, but by the awesome power of a prayer-hearing God. The spiritual preparation of the church is a vital element to success in evangelism. The first spiritual revival that led to a one-day successful public evangelism took place right after a series of ten days of earnest prayer (Acts 1: 12, 13). Whenever, in the spiritual realm, we say that something is unfeasible, impossible, or cannot work, we need to keep in mind that we have put God out of the equation. In other words, we contradict the Word of God that clearly states, "Ah, Sovereign LORD, you have made the heavens and the earth by your great power and outstretched arm. Nothing is too hard for you (Jer.32: 17)." The unique, 100% successful public evangelism recorded in the whole Bible is found in the Old Testament book of Jonah. This success was the result of prayer: "Then Jonah prayed to the LORD his God from the stomach of the fish. While I was fainting away, I remembered the LORD, and my prayer came to You, Into Your holy temple (Jon.2: 1, 7)." The New Testament does not remain silent about earnest prayer that displays the success in evangelism. Luke, in the book of Acts, reports how the disciples reacted when they were threatened not to do public evangelism: "And when they had prayed, the place where they had gathered together was shaken, and they were all filled with the Holy Spirit and began to speak the word of God with boldness (Acts 4:31)."

It is highly recommended to name a prayer coordinator with the responsibility to work closely with the series coordinator and persuade the congregation to be a house of prayer. Their role also will be that of planning, promoting, and overseeing prayer events in the church such as, special days of prayer, prayer vigils, and fasting. Teaching church members to make prayer lists and intercede for the evangelistic team is very vital. The prayer coordinator should encourage the church to pray for unity, repentance, passion for the souls, and the outpouring of the Holy Spirit. Always remember that prayer is the most important human factor in evangelism. There can be a successful reaping without good preaching but never without prayer. Earnest prayer will lead to revival and reformation in the life of the congregation that will feel the necessity of cooperating in the proclamation of the Word of God.

Principle #3: Church Involvement

The third biblical, universal principle for a successful evangelistic series is church involvement. We often rely on the ability of a well-known preacher to get success. This way of doing evangelism must be adjusted. Your excellent preacher, most of the times, does not know anyone in the community. We need to change tactics in getting church members to participate fully in the activities. A substantial rate of involvement expected can be possibly attained. We will get to this level when the church is intentional in making participation inclusive. Often times, the youth are neglected, while their participation in the preparation and implementing of a series is very critical. Not only do they have the knowledge, but also they may be channels through which other young people and their relatives will attend the meetings. Church involvement is one of the great principles to fulfill the Great Commission. The success of the early church came from the combination of the work of the Holy Spirit and the congregation's participation. Church members know the community, the targeted people, more than anybody else. Their passion for the lost and their participation can be a guarantee for success. God's work necessitates the involvement of his people in all the activities. This assertion is depicted in the Old Testament when Moses was instructed by God to build the tabernacle: "Let every skillful man among you come, and make all that the LORD has commanded. The Israelites, all the men and women, whose heart moved them to bring material for all the work, which the LORD had commanded through

Moses to be done, brought a freewill offering to the LORD (Ex. 35: 10, 29)." The 12th chapter of the book of Acts validates as well the church involvement principle in the miraculous deliverance of the apostle Peter. "Peter therefore was kept in prison: but prayer was made without ceasing of the church unto God for him. And when he had considered the thing, he came to the house of Mary the mother of John, whose surname was Mark; where many were gathered together praying (Acts 12: 5, 12)."

Principle #4: Training

The fourth biblical principle for a successful evangelistic campaign is training. Church members may eagerly want to participate in the preparation, planning, and implementing of the series; however, if they are not trained, their involvement will not bring much success. It is the responsibility of the church leadership to train and equip them for an effective participation. Sometimes, several are reluctant to cooperate just because they do not know how to do things properly. Many would be willing to work if they were taught how to do so. Before conducting an evangelistic series, the pastoral body should devote considerable time to teaching and training. Members should know how to make productive visitations, how to present a Bible study, and how to give a heartfelt invitation. At this level, every church should be a training school for their members. Since Jesus applied the Training and Equipping principle through training and mentoring, we also must do the same today. "Then Jesus sent the multitude away, and went into the house: and his disciples came unto him, saying, Declare unto us the parable of the tares of the field. He answered and said unto them, He that soweth the good seed is the Son of man; the field is the world; the good seed are the children of the kingdom; but the tares are the children of the wicked one" (Mat.13:36-43). Read verses 1through 3 for context. Training and equipping will make church members more knowledgeable, confident, and more responsible for their tasks. The prophet Hosea provides a good insight about training God's people: "My people are destroyed for lack of knowledge (Ho 4: 6a)." The apostle Paul, on his part, admonishes us to equip the saints for the work of ministry (Eph 4:12).

Principle #5: Community Outreach

The fifth biblical and dynamic principle leading to a successful evangelistic activity is Community Outreach. This principle simply means getting in touch with the vicinity of your congregation. It can also be seen as what experts call "Presence Evangelism." In preparation of an effective evangelism strategy, your church will need to establish its presence among the people through several felt-needs ministries. This principle helps to identify and satisfy some actual needs of the community. You cannot serve well those whom you ignore the basic necessities. This principle is one of the most practical pathways to the church. It covers the social, emotional, economic, and spiritual needs of the community. It also gives a statistical prospectus of the first fruits of the series. You know them, become part of them, and meet some of their needs as you win their acknowledgment. Jesus, in the Gospel of Luke, applies this principle: "And when the day began to wear away, then came the twelve, and said unto him, Send the multitude away, that they may go into the towns and country round about, and lodge, and get victuals: for we are here in a desert place. But he said unto them, Give ye them to eat. And they said, we have no more but five loaves and two fishes; except we should go and buy meat for all this people (Lk 9:12, 13)." Paul, while visiting a synagogue in Antioch, was invited to preach to the congregation: "But going on from Perga, they arrived at Pisidian Antioch, and on the Sabbath day they went into the synagogue and sat down. After the reading of the Law and the Prophets the synagogue officials sent to them, saying, 'Brethren, if you have any word of exhortation for the people, say it'" (Acts 13:14, 15).

Principle #6: Careful Planning

The sixth biblical and universal principle for a successful evangelistic series is careful planning. Evangelism does not naturally happen, even within the ministry of the church. It thus requires the organizing of an aggressive, effective, and productive work plan and the making of regular assessment to see whether the objectives are being achieved. Planning is essential for a successful evangelistic campaign. The Old Testament presents several cases of careful planning. For example, in the 13th chapter of the book of Numbers, we can read the careful planning made by Moses upon God's approval before entering Canaan: "Then the LORD spoke to Moses saying, 'Send out for yourself men so that they may spy out the land of Canaan, which I am going to give to the sons of Israel; you shall send a man from each of their fathers' tribes, everyone a leader among them.' When Moses sent them to spy out the land of Canaan, he said to them, 'Go up there into the Negev; then go up into the hill country. See what the land is like, and whether the people who live in it are strong or weak, whether they are few or many. How is the land, in which they live, is it good or bad? And how are the cities in which they live, are they like open camps or with fortifications? How is the land, is it fat or lean? Are there trees in it or not? Make an effort then to get some of the fruit of the land.' Now the time was the time of the first ripe grapes" (Num.13: 1, 2, 17-20). Jesus made allusion to this principle in the Gospel of Luke as well. He asked, "For which one of you, when he wants to build a tower, does not first sit down and calculate the cost to see if he has enough to complete it? Otherwise, when he has laid a foundation and is not able to finish, all who observe it begin to ridicule him, saying, 'This man began to build and was not able to finish'" (Lk 14: 28-30).

The planning principle requires that the church determines their target group, does ground work among them (Lk 10: 1), and decides upon an event that is appropriate to them. It is the moment to think and find out about the most convenient location, assess the feasibility and evaluate the cost of the project. The formation of various ministries or commissions and the nomination of their leaders should be taken into consideration during the planning. Make sure to offer a good-quality program, developing a clear schedule for the series, starting and ending on time. Do your best to make your guests feel comfortable as much as possible. Always remember: "Failing to plan is planning to fail."

Principle #7: Reaping
The seventh biblical principle that leads to a successful evangelistic series is reaping. In fact, it is difficult to evaluate an evangelistic effort without doing the reaping. After implementation of the six principles mentioned above, we must come to the practical aspect, which is the reaping. We have sown, planted throughout a certain period; it is now time to harvest. That is done by gathering together all those to whom we have given Bible study, our relatives, and our friends and co-workers in one specific place to listen to the preaching of the Word of God. The evangelist should be surrounded with devoted, qualified, and professional Bible workers to perform home penetration evangelism. During the series, a competent Bible teacher must be in charge of a function-

ing baptismal class. With the setting of different commissions such as, hospitality, welcome and usher, transportations, visitations, prayer, music, parking, budget, refreshments, technology, children, and so on, depending on the size of the congregation, the church is getting ready for harvesting.

Jesus recommended the "reaping" principle in the Gospel of John: "Do you not say, 'There are yet four months, and then comes the harvest'? Behold, I say to you, lift up your eyes and look on the fields, that they are white for harvest. Already he who reaps is receiving wages and is gathering fruit for life eternal; so that he who sows and he who reaps may rejoice together" (John 4: 35, 36)." And the disciples applied that principle in the second chapter of the book of Acts. "But Peter, taking his stand with the eleven, raised his voice and declared to them: 'Men of Judea and all you who live in Jerusalem, let this be known to you and give heed to my words.' And with many other words he solemnly testified and kept on exhorting them, saying, 'Be saved from this perverse generation!' So then, those who had received his word were baptized; and that day there were added about three thousand souls" (Acts 2: 14, 40-41)."

Principle #8: Christ-Focus

The eighth biblical and universal principle for a successful evangelistic series is focusing hearers on Christ, the "Christ-Focus" principle. Commissioned by Jesus to make disciples for Him, the evangelist's endeavor is to present Christ, the only source and means of salvation, to the lost. Let us have them turn their eyes to the Savior. We are called to share a biblical, Christ-centered message with the unsaved. Preachers need not to major in the preaching of the "feeling good message" to touch people's hearts and win souls for the Lord. They should not tell lies either by giving false testimonies. There is power in the name of Jesus to produce repentance and conversion. The Spirit-led Early Church, having adopted the "Christ-Focus" principle, got tremendous results and substantial growth in a relatively short period of time. This principle can be traced in the Synoptic Gospels even before Jesus started His public ministry. John the Baptist was the first preacher, who used the "Christ-Focus" principle. Several individuals believed that he was the Messiah. When the Jewish authorities from Jerusalem sent a delegation to inquire about who John the Baptist was, he clearly said that he was not Christ (Jn 1:19-20). Applying the "Christ-Focus" principle, John turned the crowd's eyes toward Jesus (Jn 1:29). The beloved disciple, John, reports that he did the same thing one day later: "The next day John was there again with two of his disciples. When he saw Jesus passing by, he said, ""Look, the Lamb of God!"" When the two disciples heard him say this, they followed Jesus (Jn 1:35-36)."

Andrew, Peter's brother was one of the two disciples who left John to follow Jesus (Jn 1:40). He shared the good news with Simon, later Peter, who also accepted the Savior. Peter, one of the most powerful preachers of the early church, had always used the "Christ-Focus" principle to win souls for Jesus. This principle, used throughout the Book of Acts, was remarkably evident in Peter's preaching ministry. He firstly applied it in the second chapter of Acts, verses 22-39, during his Pentecost sermon, where he put great emphasis on the life and ministry of Jesus. He also described the death of Jesus, His resurrection, and His exaltation. Because the entire sermon was uniquely about Jesus Christ, it was very fruitful as reported, "And with many other words he testified and exhorted them, saying, 'Be saved from this perverse generation.' Then those who gladly received his word were baptized; and that day about three thousand souls were added to them' (Acts 2: 40, 41)."

After the healing of the crippled man found in Acts 3:1-10, Peter was again to preach, using the Christ-focus principle. The Christ-centered approach of Peter's second sermon (3: 12-4: 1, 2) was as exceptional as the first. He directed the crowd's attention away from them (Peter and John) to the Christ, whom we are supposed to tell the unsaved about. The "Christ-focus" principle shows our vulnerability and teaches us humility. It helps us to give God all the credit. It was not by chance that Peter turned people toward Jesus. He recognizes his human frailty by admitting only Jesus can touch people's hearts and perform miracles. Having lifted the name of Jesus on high, the outcome was amazing, "However, many of those who heard the word believed; and the number of the men came to be about five thousand (Acts 4: 4)." Peter also had a wonderful result at Cornelius' house after using his Christ-centered method. Read Acts 10:34-48. Luke reports that Philip, the deacon-evangelist, used the "Christ-Focus" principle as well: "Then Philip began with that very passage of Scripture and told him the good news about Jesus (Ac 8:35)."

Paul, for not yet fully applying this principle in his speech (Acts 17: 22-33), had little success in Athens: "However, some men joined him and believed, among them Dionysius the Areopagite, a woman named Damaris, and others with them"

(Acts 17: 34). However, realizing its importance in Corinth, he saw many souls giving their lives to Jesus: "Then Crispus, the ruler of the synagogue, believed on the Lord with all his household. And many of the Corinthians, hearing, believed and were baptized (Acts 18: 8)". Paul championed the "Christ-focus" principle throughout his entire ministry, in particular among the Corinthians, "For I determined not to know anything among you except Jesus Christ and Him crucified (1 Cor.2: 2)."

Principle #9: Holy Spirit

The ninth biblical and indispensable principle for a successful evangelism strategy is the claiming of the Holy Spirit. It is crucial to remember that evangelism is not a human endeavor. We cannot do it on our own. Evangelism is too big; it cannot be accomplished in human strength. There is nothing we can do in the evangelism realm without the power of the Holy Spirit, as stated by Jesus in Acts 1: 8. Before the launching of their evangelistic series, the early church made all necessary adjustments, confessed their mistakes, and received the Holy Spirit. No matter how excellent an evangelist may be, conversion and baptism remain the work of the Holy Spirit. Jesus tells His disciples to wait until they receive this power (Ac 1:8; Lk 24: 47-59). Today's church needs to experience the presence and empowerment of the Spirit before initiating any evangelistic activity. Evangelism in all its aspects is the work of the awesome power of the Holy Spirit. Speaking of Jesus: "And He said to them, 'Go, and make disciples of all nations, baptizing them in the name of the Father and of the Son and of the Holy Spirit, teaching them to observe all things that I commanded you. Behold, I am with you always, even to the end of the age (Mat.28:19-20)."

Whenever someone gets involved in evangelism, they need to claim the power of the Holy Spirit. God has already promised and made this power available to us. In fact, the Lord has never called a soldier in the field without equipping them. Elisha received a double portion of Elijah's Spirit upon his God-calling. John the Baptist, who had the mission of preparing the way for Christ, got the Holy Spirit while he was in the womb of his mother. As we prepare Jesus' second return, we also must and can be filled with the Holy Spirit if we claim him. Our responsibility is simply to share the message as clearly and lovingly as we can, asking the Spirit to apply it in His own way and time. Only the Holy Spirit can bring conviction and conversion. Keep in mind that even Jesus had to be baptized with the Holy Spirit before beginning his earthly ministry!

Principle #10: Baptism

The tenth biblical principle for a successful evangelistic series is Baptism. One of the main purposes of evangelism is to lead people to the Lordship of Jesus as their personal Savior through baptism as shown in Acts 2: 41. We cannot spend all our time talking to people about the Savior without encouraging them to publicly show their allegiance to Him. Once they believe in Christ as the Son of God, the next step is baptism. Jesus is clear about this principle in all the gospels, which is an integral component of the Great commission. In the Gospel of Matthew, Jesus equates baptism as a just thing to do (Mt. 3: 15). Baptism reveals the identity of the baptized. For instance, before His baptism, nobody except his parents knew really who Jesus was; however, His identification, as Beloved Son of God, was made public right after being baptized (Mt. 3: 17). Christ unambiguously shows the salvific aspect of that principle in the Gospel of Mark. And He said to them, "Go into all the world and preach the gospel to every creature. He who believes and is baptized will be saved; but he who does not believe will be condemned (Mark 16: 15, 16)." Baptism is the doorway to the fellowship of the church and the clear initiation to a discipleship lifestyle. As an official induction to the family of God, baptism must be carefully prepared to receive the neophytes. People do not need to wait for ages before getting baptized. The Bible does not teach its postponement. Some postulants argue that they get to understand thoroughly the Bible before being baptized. This thought is incorrect. In fact, if someone wishes to have comprehension of the Word, they need to get baptized for the forgiveness of their sins and the reception of the Holy Spirit (Acts 2: 38) that will explain the scriptural truths. Whenever a decision is confirmed, baptism is possible during the day or at night. The cases of the Ethiopian Eunuch and of the jailer of Philippi reported in the book of Acts are respectively critical evidences that baptism should not be delayed (Acts 8: 34-39; 16: 30-33). One cannot be a committed and responsible disciple without following Christ's example and instruction (Mat.3: 13-16; 28: 19).

It is noteworthy to tell that the very first time we have put all these principles into application in our church was in August 1999. As a result, 48 people got baptized during the month in a congregation that had never baptized over 15 believers yearly. In addition to these baptisms, follow-up studies were conducted with about 30 postulants who were not fully decided at the conclusion of the series.

It is critical to underline that the work of evangelism does not end at baptism. Baptism is just the beginning of the new believer's spiritual journey. Most churches fall short at this level. Evangelism is a "going concern" activity; it continues until new converts are trained to share their faith and be ready for the Second Coming of Christ. People are not baptized to become church members for a short period of time. They give their lives to Jesus to become Disciples of Christ as per the Savior's instruction found in the Gospel of Matthew: "Make disciples of all the nations, baptizing them in the name of the Father and of the Son and of the Holy Spirit, teaching them to observe all things that I have commanded you (Mt 28: 19b, 20a)." Now, what is next after an individual gives their life to the Lordship of Jesus Christ through baptism? Luke, in the book of Acts, gives a valuable insight. "They were continually devoting themselves to the apostles' teaching and to fellowship, to the breaking of bread and to prayer (Acts 2: 42). The next chapter will indicate a clear biblical rule, retention (Jn 15:16), as how to retain new converts and make them become disciples.

TIPS FOR SIMPLE BUT INTENTIONAL EVANGELISM

Visiting and assisting a grieving family	Helping others carry their grocery bags
Giving a cooking class at the church	Presenting a finance seminar
Watching games with neighbors	Kindly opening and holding doors for…
Organizing after-school programs	Offering a health/stress free seminar
Watching over kids or elderly for friends	Inviting frends and neighbors to church
Organizing back to school programs	Offering a drug/tobacco free seminar
Mowing the lawn of your neighbor	Praying by names for friends/neighbors
Presenting a family seminar	Having a children's choir perform for the sick

1   Ellen G. White, *The Ministry of Healing* (Nampa, ID: Pacific Press Publishing Association, 2003), 143.

CHAPTER FIVE
RETENTION: KEEPING THEM

This chapter will exhibit two main points. The first point underlines the commitment of the newly baptized to Christ. It consists of encouraging the new converts to remain in the church for further instructions in order to resist the Devil's attacks and progress in their relationship with Jesus. The second point aims at reminding church leadership of their duty to assimilate and keep the new believers so they can become disciples, as stated by Jesus in Matthew 28:19. In both cases, the cooperation of new converts is extremely critical.

One of the greatest challenges we have as a church is the retention of members, both new and regular members. They need to be constantly reaffirmed in Christ. When the church fails to nurture the recently converted, they fail in complying with the mission. The conservation, or preservation, or Retention of church members (mainly New Converts) is not optional but a direct command from our Lord Jesus Christ. The Savior unambiguously made this claim plain in the Gospel of John, saying: "I have chosen you and ordained you, that you should go and bring forth fruit, and that your fruit should remain" (John 15:16).

The Master really knew what He meant when He exhorted the disciples that their fruit should remain. There is a huge difference in the lives of those who leave the church with those who remain. Throughout my Christian journey and my professional life, this discrepancy becomes obvious. Some families do well when they stay and get involved in church activities. Others are backward as they leave and do not participate. My extended family bears witness to these lamentable scenarios. Siblings and cousins are victims of leaving the church. One of the main reasons for this early exit is deficiency in maturity generated by a lack of teaching, training, and mentoring new converts in addition to a poor knowledge of the Bible, and particularly of Jesus Christ.

My most shocking experience of people leaving the church soon after conversion happened in 1994. In April 1994, the church organized an evangelistic series on the book of Revelation. At the end of the campaign, two hundred and fifty-three persons gave their lives to Jesus through baptism. About six months later, less than 15% of those new converts remained in the church. Because they were ignorant of the basic teachings of God's word and did not have a mature relation with Jesus, they just left a few months later. Being a member of the visitations committee gave me the opportunity to meet with people who became hostile to the gospel. It was an appalling experience.

Another disastrous ecclesiastical spiritual experience was that of an ex-member of another church that I had attended. In August 1999, the church held an evangelistic series for one month. Three days before concluding the campaign, a young man, possessed by an evil spirit, came to church. After spending quality time in prayer, healing occurred by the power of the Holy Spirit. Coming into his good sense, he accepted Jesus as his personal Savior and got baptized on Saturday, September 4, 1999. It was an amazing event, and his mother also received baptism on that day. She still attends the church.

About four months later, this young man discontinued attending the post-baptismal class organized for new converts, went to a dance club, and got sick. The elders of the church went to visit him, prayed for him, and he was healed. However, before leaving his house, one of the elders told him expressly not to go to such places anymore. He did not follow the elder's instruction. A few months after his recovery, he left the church, enjoyed his life, and cut all contacts with the church officials. Unfortunately, three years later, he passed away.

There have been several difficult times in my life, such as experiencing parental deaths unexpectedly. There have been many challenges in my spiritual journey. However, learning the basic principles of a Christian life, Christ, my special friend since my baptism, compels me to remain in church and actively participate in all activities. A church where most members involve in the ministries cannot be stagnant or regressive. It will grow and remain healthy. The members, in this case, will build up better relationships with God and with one another. When they are members of the same ministry and work together, they know each other better and have the opportunity to develop a genuine Christian friendship.

My personal and professional life compared to that of those who have left the church shortly after their baptism has led me to develop a Christ-based discipleship program. Through this program, new converts will find no better place than the church. They will gain confidence, participate in missionary activities, and remain in church until Christ returns. As an experienced associate discipleship pastor, those who are keenly involved in church activities make me confident about the feasibility of this project. The church exists to better people's lives and to prepare them for eternity. During the flood, only those who were inside the ark were saved. It thus becomes imperative for new converts to remain in the church as they invite others to join them. Leaving the church has eternal consequences. In general, those who cut themselves from the fellowship of the saints do not have a healthy relation with God as well.

This project aims at proposing a plan that can help every new believer to develop a constant, personal, and spiritual relationship with Jesus by actively engaging in the work of the Master. Once each new convert in the church is taught the accounting principle of a "going concern," which means they shall stay in business with and for Christ permanently, they will intentionally remain committed to the Lord Jesus until He comes back. Over the years, baptism occurred for many people; however, few remain in the church. It is really time to close the back door! The best way to do that is to transform new converts from members to disciples.

Church's Duty

Imagine yourself going fishing and that all the fish you have caught disappear! What satisfaction will you get in the end? Too often, the church sees baptism as the final result of evangelism. An evangelism strategy will be successful only when new converts remain in the church to be instructed as per Jesus' command and become themselves disciples and disciple-makers until they are introduced to Christ. In other terms, there is no discipleship without member retention. We have sought, and have found them. It is now our responsibility to keep them, to teach them so they can become mature disciples. One of the key principles to keep in mind at this stage is to remember that the Bible views them as babies in the faith. "Therefore, laying aside all malice, all deceit, hypocrisy, envy, and all evil speaking, as newborn babies, desire the pure milk of the word, that you may grow thereby" (1 Pt. 2: 1, 2). As such, they must be nurtured. How can that happen if they do not remain in the church?

From 1994 through 2013, I conducted four surveys on member retention among new converts in two countries. One survey was outside the United States and three others in three different states in the U.S. among one ethnic group. The objective has always been to find out the reasons why these new converts leave the church so quickly after their baptism. I have interviewed 303 individuals, of which 197 have left the church in less than a year of their commitment to following Christ. Every new convert has been asked the same question. Could you give at least three-five reasons why you have left the church so quickly after your baptism? I have obtained several different responses that I have grouped in ten categories. To make the study easy, the first five categories with higher frequency were selected for evaluation. The first category of respondents (96) said they left because of lack of love. The second group (87) mentioned that they did not really understand the Bible. The third group (78) advanced that ministering to others is too challenging. The fourth category (69) said they gave up because of a lack of training. And finally, the fifth group (44) testified that they lost their former friends and that it was difficult for them to get new ones. The last five groups with lower frequency were as follows: family opposition (39), loss of job/friends (37), non-involvement in church (30), decision naively made (27), and new jargon/ old members' strange behavior (24).

Seven Critical Keys to Successful Retention

The most important factor in retaining new converts is connecting them to Christ. That must begin during the initial encounter with the person, be emphasized throughout the evangelistic series, and continue after their incorporation. Preachers have to be intentional in presenting Christ-centered sermons, so that people may turn their eyes upon Jesus. Moreover, the church must cultivate a policy of inclusion. This inclusive nature should lead the church in an intentional process of discipling all new believers who enter the church. Retention does not happen automatically or by chance. It is the church's responsibility to be intentional and deliberate in retaining members. There must exist within the congregation a ministry that puts great emphasis on retention. There is no progression and or production evangelism without member retention. Thus, the decisive task of the church is to create a healthy environment for welcoming new converts so they can attain Christian maturity. Keeping the new believers is an integral part of the Great Commission; therefore, careful plan and preparation should precede the arrival of new converts in the church.

Based on the results of the surveys and considering the fact that the Bible views new converts as babies in faith, and also as per our church life experience, we would like to propose some crucial keys that can lead to a vital, constant relationship with Jesus and a successful retention program. The first four keys will display the analogy of a babe's fundamental needs for growth as means of aiding new converts to develop a living connection with Christ.

Key #1: Love (Fellowship)
As highly mentioned by the respondents in the surveys, love is a critical key in keeping new converts in the church. It is one of the fundamental needs that can facilitate the growth of a babe. The new believer must see it and feel it through genuine fellowship. David understood that so well when he wrote, "Behold, how good and how pleasant it is for brethren to dwell together in unity! It is like the precious ointment upon the head that ran down upon the beard, even Aaron's beard: that went down to the skirts of his garments; as the dew of Hermon, and as the dew that descended upon the mountains of Zion: for there the LORD commanded the blessing, even life for evermore (Ps.133: 1-3)." This bonding must start before the series through friendship evangelism. This companionship has to be exercised during the campaign by warm welcome and good manners. This fellowship should continue after the series, as demonstrated in the early church. Luke, based on the behavior of the newly baptized at Pentecost, wrote, "And they continued steadfastly in the apostles' doctrine and fellowship, and in breaking of bread, and in prayers (Acts 2:42)."

Love, the core teaching of Christ's ministry, is a fundamental principle in life. Indeed, the whole gospel is focused on that great, eternal principle, love for God and love for our neighbor. Jesus made it a condition sine qua non as how to prove to others that we are His disciples. "By this all will know that you are my disciples, if you have love for one another (Jn 13:35)." If the church really wants to make disciples, we must be intentional in retaining them by unconditionally loving them. Either we love them like Christ to transform them into disciples, or we will lose them.

Key #2: Air (Prayer)

A babe, to fully develop, does need fresh air. Alike, to grow in their spiritual journey, new converts necessitate prayer. Not only do we have to pray for and with them, but also teach them how to pray. We generally say that we pray for them. However, we often forget to teach them how to do so with the presuppositions they knew that beforehand. This way of thinking gets to be corrected. The Bible calls them "babies," let us consider them as such. We must teach them to pray in order to develop and maintain a constant relationship with Jesus through personal devotion, family worship, and small group meetings. We are supposed to instruct them that prayer should be a lifestyle for all Christians. We have already talked about the importance of prayer in the previous chapter; we will go over it again in chapter ten. However, it is worth telling new converts that most great victories in the spiritual realm and material world are the results of prayer. The prophet Daniel had the custom of praying three times a day. "Now when Daniel knew that the writing was signed, he went home. And in his upper room, with his windows open toward Jerusalem, he knelt down on his knees three times that day, and prayed and gave thanks before his God, as was his custom since early days (Da.6: 10)." Have our new believers imitate Christ's prayer life pattern. Christ had a time and a place to regularly pray. Jesus started his day with prayer: "Now in the morning, having risen a long while before daylight, He went out and departed to a solitary place; and there He prayed (Mk.1: 35)." The Savior also prayed with and for others (Lk 9: 28, 22:31). It is our duty to urge them to follow Paul's advice found in his first letter to Thessalonica, "pray without ceasing (1 Thess. 5:17)."

Key #3: Food (the Word of God)

Food is an indispensable element in the development of all human beings, more particularly in the growth of a babe. For the new convert, that food, taken in a spiritual context, represents the Word of God. It is crucial that the church organizes special Bible study classes for the newly converted in order to know more about Jesus. As new converts need material food to sustain them physically, they must eat spiritual food as well to stand spiritually. New converts must be taught and encouraged to regularly study the Bible. Christ unequivocally puts emphasis on the importance of searching the Scriptures as the best and right way to know Him. The beloved disciple, reporting in his gospel the words of Jesus, writes, "You search the Scriptures, for in them you think you have eternal life; and these are they which testify of Me (John 5: 39)." Indeed, the whole Bible (Old Testament and New Testament) is all about Jesus Christ. In His encounter with two of His disciples on the Road of Emmaus after the crucifixion, Jesus clearly teaches that Scriptures are to take precedence over personal experiences. Instead of revealing Himself to the two men, He rather gave them a Bible study by directing their attention on the Scriptures. He later used the same method to open the spiritual eyes of the other ten (Thomas was absent) disciples who were hiding out of sight for fear of the Jews (see John 20:19). Luke reports this Bible study twice in his Gospel (Lk 24: 25-27, 44-47).

A living connection with Jesus requires systematic study of the Scriptures, which is a sure defense against the enemy and his deceptions. Because He hid the Word of God in His heart, Jesus was able to overcome the temptations of the Devil in the wilderness with a clear "It is written" (Mt 4: 1-10). To grow spiritually and walk in the light, new converts must take time to study the Word. The author of the longest chapter in the Bible expresses this assertion convincingly in the book of Psalms: "Your word is a lamp to my feet and a light to my path (Ps 119: 105)." When one accepts Jesus as their personal Savior, they claim themselves enemies of sin. The most accurate way to resist against sin is revealed through the keeping of the Word of God in one's heart (Ps 119: 11). Thus, feeding themselves with the Word indicates new converts' decision to know Christ more and to maintain a vital relationship with Him. No other piece of literature, or any scientific book, but only the Word of God has the power to change people's lives. We must teach them the importance of the Scriptures and encourage them to study the Word if we really want to keep them in the church.

Key #4: Exercise or Physical activity (Witnessing/Mission)
Imagine how frustrating it can be to notice that your babe cannot sit, stand, walk, or move at all! Most experts advance that physical activity plays a

crucial role in a child's general development: motor skills, cognitive development, psychological well-being, physical abilities, and emotional maturity. The sooner a child understands the importance of physical activity, the more likely they are to adopt a long-term healthy lifestyle. Let us now view this situation on a different or spiritual angle since the Bible calls new converts "babies" in faith. Since inactivity is the cause of many health problems among children, it is the church's responsibility to make new converts active. One of the main ways to initiate their bustle is to involve them in witnessing or missionary activities according to the gift that each has been given. If we want to retain our new converts, we must start their assimilation right after baptism.

Several old church members argue that new converts get to wait a reasonable period of time before their involvement in church's activities. They generally base their rationale on the recommendation of the apostle Paul to Timothy inserted in first Timothy 3:6. However, if the church intentionally wants to keep the new believers, they should not delay their involvement in ministry. The problem here is the fact that the church is not ready in their preparation to assimilate or incorporate new converts. I remember, when my wife discovered she was pregnant with our first son, how quickly she started preparing his coming. A child's birth is a process, which begins long before the child's arrival in the world and continues long thereafter. Similarly, as in the physical birth process, the plan to retain new converts should begin before they arrive. The most important thing is that the church has to set a retention plan even before they come in.

At this juncture, we are not talking about holding high positions in church, such as being a board member, head of department, and so on. Our point is to put these new converts at work. Assimilation or involvement can be made through various ministries. A few new believers, for example, may become members of a team that makes visits in hospitals, nursing homes, and prisons. Some may be affiliated with prayer ministry, literature distribution, and hospitality ministry. Others may join a singing group, Bible reading team, and so on. I cannot forget how happy a 49-year-old woman was when, two weeks after her baptism, she was introduced as a server to the cafeteria team. Two years later, she became the assistant manager of the kitchen, and she still follows Christ and serves the church on many other levels.

Key #5: Friendship

In the findings of the surveys conducted, one of the key reasons new converts leave the church early is lack or absence of meaningful friendships. Experts in the church-growth movement have discovered through years of research that the most frequent reason why people join the church for the first time is the influence of friends or relatives. At the same token, if this important factor constitutes a positive way to bring people in, it must also be used as a means of preventing the new members from leaving through the back door. There is within each new believer a desire to belong, to feel secure, to love, and to be loved in their new community. One of the challenges to attaining these needs is the failure of the church to be intentional in creating structures and ways for retaining members. If they do not find or experience friendships in their new congregation, they will certainly look for it somewhere else, mostly among their former, unsaved friends. Some experts advance that each new convert should be able to identify at least seven friends in the church within the first six months. Friendships appear to be the strongest bond cementing new converts to their congregation

The purpose of friendships is to establish and develop spiritual and social relationships. We should always remember that the Bible calls new converts "babies" in the faith. As a result, teaching them meaningful ways to make friends should be on the priorities' list of the church. Some new converts join the church through other means than friends and relatives; therefore, the church has a moral and spiritual obligation to create ministries within which these new converts can establish lasting friendships. One of the best ways to help new members make new friends is to involve them in friendship-building activities of the church. To be effective, friendship needs to be balanced. Some churches put more emphasis on its spiritual aspect and neglect the social dimension. In this distressful society, recreation or social activities among church members play a crucial role in keeping them jointly. These help them to put aside the vicissitudes and the challenges of life to spend some quality time together and better know each other. This is the best occasion for them to build friendships. Activity and friendships are two key elements to retain new converts in church.

During a Saturday night recreation, four church members were playing dominoes. It was interesting to hear the testimonial of a new convert sharing his joy to be a member of the family of God. "I was a little bit discouraged at home. But, I suddenly became happy when my friend called and told me there were games at the church. It is now a different setting. I am playing with godly friends in a secure environment. I feel good!" Christian friendship produces respect, trust, bonds, and encouragement. Friendship plays an invaluable role in keeping a church together. The stronger the relationships are, the more spiritual the congregation becomes, and the more they display God's love message to the world.

Key #6: Evangelistic Small Groups
The Evangelistic Small Groups ministry is one of the most basic ways to retain new converts in the church. It facilitates their assimilation and integration and provides a deep sense of belonging. It is one of the key factors that will help the church fulfill its internal and external mission. The Evangelistic Small Groups setting generates a two-fold purpose with multiple facets of growth for the new convert. It firstly strengthens and makes them feel at home, and secondly empowers them to share the good news with the lost. This Evangelistic Small Groups ministry may look different from the traditional ones. It consists in creating a friendly environment where new converts can build strong and healthy relationships, and also evangelize to people who would be more unlikely to attend a church meeting. Without undermining the internal growth of the recent believers, we want the setting to take an evangelistic approach as well, which is evangelism outside the box. In short, the Evangelistic Small Groups ministry pursues two main goals. First, it facilitates the strengthening of the new convert to become mature disciples through prayer, Bible study, and fellowship. And secondly, it encourages the new convert to develop strong and friendly relationships with non-believers in a more private setting to witness to them. This is really the place for new believers to keep their fire burning for Christ.

The model is simple but very significant. It is built on 5Ws: Welcome, Word, Worship, Witnessing, and Wasting time together (Fellowship). Have at least two new converts become members of an Evangelistic Small Group where five to ten church members would be encouraged to minister in their neighborhood. Each small group will comprise of a leader, a co-leader, a host, and a secretary. They will find a meeting time suitable to them during the week. The key thing is to have at least one empty chair that should be filled by a non member. Every person attending the group should be interested in inviting or bringing new people. The meeting will have at least three sections.

In the first section (Welcome), opportunity is given to each member of the cell to tell about their past week's experience, positive or negative, sharing their joy with others. During the suggested twenty minutes allotted, any special occasion related to member life should be granted specific attention. We must begin the program at the point of people's interest and need; in other words, we ought to use a felt-need approach. During the second part (Word and Worship), time is reserved for studying the Bible and adoration. It can also be a heartfelt worship in combining authenticity and vulnerability with a genuine experience of God's presence. We need to worship in ways that are accessible to pre-Christians. Members should be able to give their inputs. 45 minutes of study will be suitable. And the third section (Wasting time together and Witnessing) includes the Fellowship time where members joyfully take their collation, and the commitment time as they promise to do mission and share their new learning. Sharing the meal to start the meeting is also a very good option. At the end of this section, members should feel comfortable to request any kind of service they might need during the coming days. For instance, someone may need to be taken to the doctor or dropped at the airport.

This Small Group ministry provides a sense of belonging and community. Old members and new converts build good and healthy relationships. They worship God, study the Scriptures together, and fellowship with one another. The most interesting aspect of this blending is the fact they reach out to the lost in a very productive way. There is a high probability to retain new converts that are members of a Small Group ministry. However, those who are not involved in any kinds of Small Groups' activities are vulnerable and more likely to leave the church. There may be different types of Small Group ministries. For example, those who share the same hobbies or profession can be grouped together. The bottom line is that the church must be intentional in building these small groups even before new converts come. In the end, as important as it is, the Small Groups ministry does not replace church's regular meetings and should not operate in parallel with the official and planned activities in the church.

Key #7: Pastoral Visitation

Being intentional in retaining new converts requires the participation and accountability of the entire community of faith. However, pastoral visits cannot be replaced by what others do. It is one of the main components of the pastoral care initiative. Few people nowadays would ignore that we are living in a very high-tech society where, with a simple device, one can reach out to several individuals at the same time and almost everywhere. As per my experience in the field of retention, I have discovered that electronic tools cannot substitute for pastoral visits. Pastoral visitation can be made in person and/or by other means such as, telephone, internet, and so on. A pastor should develop the habit of visiting their church members, in particular new converts. This is a good moment to get acquainted with them, to have a better idea of who and what they are. You do not need to wait for a special occasion to cause you to visit them. They are new and ignore who you are. They are uncomfortable with talking to you about their needs and problems they actually face at home, at work, or even at church. Clergy should take time to visit new converts to give them a sense of belonging to a family that cares for them, listens to them, and empathizes with them.

In addition to visiting them in person, pastors should also cultivate the habit of calling and taking calls from their members. Many politicians answer their calls. Why should a pastor be afraid of answering their phone? You are in business of saving souls for the Lord; if you cannot answer right away, have the courtesy to return the call as soon as you can. I am not trying to make you feel guilty. I just want to bring the importance of this crucial principle at your attention. To corroborate this fact, read the three testimonials below:

In the summer of 2000, while visiting the recent baptized of the church, an elder and I found out that two new converts (a young man and a young woman in their twenties) shared the same home. They lived together without getting married. We talked to them and explained to them that the Bible prohibits this type of cohabitation. We discovered that they loved one another; however, they thought they needed more time to get ready for the wedding. The situation was brought to the attention of the senior pastor who had several séances of counseling with them. They decided to get married but did not have funds enough for the reception. As the case was shared with the church's board, they voted for a substantial aid. The pastor celebrated the wedding in the church, and the fellowship hall was packed with friends and family members while the deaconesses and the hospitality committee offered an unforgettable reception. This pastoral visitation helped them to live in harmony with the Word of God, prevented discrediting the church, and caused them to remain in the church to serve the Lord.

In July 2001, a couple, attending an evangelistic series in our church, accepted the message, and gave their lives to Christ through baptism. Two months later, it was about 10:30 P.M., the husband called and told me to come over immediately, because his wife was about to hurt him with a knife. "You probably think I should have told him to call the police, don't you? But, it was not that simple. The wife, less than a year before, has been jailed for domestic violence. My wife and I went to their home and got there by 11:15. We carefully listened to them and prayed with them. With the help of the Holy Spirit, before we left the problem was solved, and they are still attending the same church. The wife currently manages a free food distribution ministry. Praise the Lord! Can you think what could have happened if I did not pick up the call?

In August 2012, having participated in a series as a Bible worker, I had the privilege to study with several postulants. Being responsible for the Bible study class, I got to get acquainted with many of the baptismal candidates. The Holy Spirit had convinced a lot of them, and thirty-six were baptized. I usually keep two lists after a series: the list of new converts and that of those in the valley of decision for follow-up studies. About four months later, I called one of the newly baptized, a single mother with a handicapped child, encouraged her to remain in Christ, and prayed with her. At the end of the conversation, she said, "Pastor, the Lord had you visit with me, because just hours before you called me, I was contemplating killing myself." A timely phone call saves a life. Think about that!

New converts, losing their jobs because of their new faith, need to hear words of comfort and receive letters from their pastor enabling them to maintain or regain their employment. Many of them are facing family challenges due to their acceptance of Christ. Some feel discouraged by the former members' attitudes and aptitudes, who expect the new believers to behave like them. While some complain about their non-involvement in the church's life, others refuse to participate. The pastor, though he should not play the role of a babysitter, is the key person to deal with these issues. He therefore must develop the habit of visiting his new believers in order to facilitate their assimilation and retention in the church.

Early Church's Legacy

God cares for his church and leaves no room for speculation about retaining new converts. In addition to the seven keys previously mentioned, the book of Acts displays several distinctive marks leading to a successful retention model. If we want our new believers to be connected to Christ and faithfully remain in church, we should imitate the model applied in the early church. Among the pertinent characteristics found in that book for a successful retention program, John Stott enumerates four of them in *The Message of Acts* as a result of the Pentecost: "(a) the early church was a learning church. The very first evidence Luke mentions of the Spirit's presence in the church is that they devoted themselves to the apostles' teachings. (b) The early church was a loving church. They devoted themselves to the fellowship. This fellowship bears witness to the common life of the church in two senses. First, it expresses what we share in together. This is God Himself. Secondly, the fellowship also expresses what we share out together, what we give as well as what we receive. (c) The early church was a worshipping church. They devoted themselves to the breaking of bread and to prayer (Ac 2:42). That is, their fellowship was expressed not only in caring for each other, but in corporate worship too. (d) The early church was an evangelistic church. They were engaged in continuous evangelism."[1]

Moreover, the early church was a praying church (Ac 1: 14; 4: 23-31). They were also a mission driven, outward-focused and evangelistic minded church (Ac 2:47b). Because they invited non-believers in their meetings, the Lord, through their preaching, added daily to them those who were being saved. Even persecution could not prevent them from preaching the Word (Ac 8:4-5). The early church was a God-fearing church; as a result, the Lord performed signs and wonders among them through the apostles (Ac 2: 43). Finally, the early church was a Spirit-filled church (Ac 2: 4; 4: 31, 6:3, 10). God does not change. Through the work of the Holy Spirit, today's church can not only retain their new converts but also transform them into disciples by building loving and Christ-like relationships. The good news is that the Holy Spirit is available and wants to perform this task. We just have to claim Him! Let Him take control and the leading of God's church.

Reflective Retention Tips
QUESTION: How did the Retention program of the Early Church go?
ANSWER: It went **WELL**.
W: Worshipping together (Ac 2: 42, 46, 47a)
E: Evangelizing daily (Ac 2: 47b)
L: Loving one another (Ac 2: 42, 45, 44)
L: Learning continuously (Ac 2: 42a)

Do you want to keep your new believers and make them disciples?
Yes. Pray and Have your church go **WELL** as well.

1:   John R. W. Stott, *The Message of Acts: The Spirit, the Church, and the World* (Downers Grove, IL: Inter-Varsity Press, 1994), 82-87.

CHAPTER SIX

DISCIPLESHIP: MAKING THEM DISCIPLES

Jesus' clear and final mandate to the disciples is unequivocally inserted in the 28th chapter of the Gospel of Matthew. The command, "Make disciples," is crystal clear: "Go therefore and make disciples of all the nations, baptizing them in the name of the Father and of the Son and of the Holy Spirit, teaching them to observe all things that I have commanded you; and lo, I am with you always, even to the end of the age (Mat.28: 19, 20)." It is paramount for the church to fully understand the core message of the Master's Great Commission. Referring to the original Greek rendition is very helpful in grasping the central message of the passage, which is to "make disciples." The original Greek version (transliteration) showcases one verb (matheteusate) from the root mathetes meaning to disciple (to make a disciple), and three participles (poreuthentes, baptizontes, and didaskontes), respectively translated as going, baptizing, and teaching. These participles, called participles of means, are inseparably connected with the main verb (disciple). It is responsible to note that there is no noun connected with the verb disciple in the Greek, but, it is also obvious that when you disciple new believers, they become disciples. Going (evangelizing or sharing the gospel with the lost), baptizing, and teaching them are the means or ways to disciple the newly baptized, or make them disciples. You may find it difficult, but the main idea of the passage is making disciples. In other words, making disciples is central to God's plan and vision to save the human race.

I want you to catch Jesus' explicit command displayed in His final talk with the disciples before His ascension. As God's representative and ambassador on earth, the church is called not to make members but disciples. In other words, the purpose of the Church as the body of Christ is to intentionally disciple the neophytes, so that they continue in an active and fruitful relationship with Christ and His Church. To better understand the mandate, "Make disciples," let us consider a simple illustration. My wife is an excellent cake-maker. However, before she can make a cake, she has to follow a lot of steps, which one is not going to see in the finished product. She must mix together several ingredients (flour, sugar, egg, butter, milk, and so on), bake them at a regular temperature, and get the final product, which is the cake. That is exactly the same way you make disciples: going (sharing the good news with someone), baptizing the believer, and teaching them to observe Christ's instructions. The four Greek words are not used to impress those who are unfamiliar with the Greek language. Their appearance is to shed light on the generally misinterpreted or misunderstood declaration of Jesus inserted in Mt. 28:19, 20. If we do not grasp the message intended, we will render the Great Commission's fulfillment very difficult and even impossible.

As per the light shed on the passage, one can now agree that making disciples requires several steps. Though there may be many more, Matthew 28: 19-20 suggests at least three steps in the process of discipling the new believers or making them disciples. These three ways are: going, baptizing, and teaching. In addition to these tri-prerequisites to discipleship, another crucial element, retention, was considered. Great emphasis has been put on these principles in the two previous chapters. (1) Going, seen as evangelism in an ongoing process wherever one may be, is the initial stage in making disciples. This participle with imperative force linked to the verbal command (disciple) displays intentionality in going out to share the good news with all: relatives, friends, neighbors, co-workers, and foreigners, and make them disciples. (2) Baptizing, seen as the entrance door to God's family, is the public acceptance of Jesus as Lord and Savior. Retention has been also considered in order to facilitate new converts' enrollment to the lifetime school of discipleship. (3) Teaching, one of the most important stages in the making of disciples, has been most of the times overlooked. This may be the result of neglect or ignorance. Most churches make good grades in going and in baptizing but poorly score in teaching. Why? The reason is obvious: they generally equate baptism to the end of the spiritual journey of the neophytes. They thus neglect the teaching component of the Great Commission.

Taken etymologically, the word disciple means learner, pupil…, as such, there is no student without teaching. It is inconceivable to disciple or to make disciples without taking the time to teach them as recommended by Jesus (Mt.28: 20). In the Gospel of Mark, Jesus told two disciples to follow Him and He would make them fishers of men (Mk 1: 17). What did the Master mean? He simply told these two fishermen that He would disciple them; in other terms, He would teach them how to share the good news with other human beings. Do not worry, he probably said to Simon and Andrew, "You will spend three years at my school, and I will teach you what you need to get the work done." Teaching is a vital part in making disciples. Jesus devoted much of His time in the teaching ministry. It is a grave error not to follow Christ's example in this. In then Christ's school of discipleship, there were certainly some other requirements to satisfy before becoming a mature disciple and/or a discipler. However, teaching had played a critical role in the process of discipling. Christ did it before and after the resurrection, the early church made teaching an integral part of its curriculum; for new converts were devoted to the teachings of the apostles. Paul and Barnabas practiced it, and the apostle Paul exhorted the young pastor Timothy to do the same. As shown in chapters one and two, teaching has always been a critical component for the church in the process of making disciples. The most important thing for today's church is to find out and imitate Jesus' strategy and method of making disciples. Without intentional teaching, the Great Commission is incomplete.

Christ's Method of Making Disciples

Christ has always set examples. He does not change and cannot contradict himself. He would never ask His disciples to make disciples without giving clear examples or insights as how to do so. When it comes to reaching people, Jesus certainly had a method. One of the pioneers of the Seventh-Day Adventist Church puts it this way: "Christ's method alone will give true success in reaching the people. The Saviour mingled with men as one who desired their good. He showed His sympathy for them, ministered to their needs, and won their confidence. Then He bade them, "Follow Me.""[iii] If Christ had a method to reach the people, he must surely have a method to make disciples as well. It is worth telling that Jesus had more than twelve, seventy, or one hundred and twenty followers. However, the Synoptic Gospels report Jesus' final mandate as being given to the eleven disciples after Judas' suicide. This helps us understand that the Master had selected a specific group among His followers to become His disciples. It is unquestionable that all Jesus' followers were not disciples. We may at this point infer that Jesus used a sorting method in choosing those who would become His disciples. The selective pattern given in the Great Commission might have been the same He employed in making disciples. The pattern is as follows. He preached the Word to all people. "Now after John was put in prison, Jesus came to Galilee, preaching the gospel of the kingdom of God, and saying, ""The time is fulfilled, and the kingdom of God is at hand. Repent, and believe in the gospel""" (Mk 1: 14, 15)." Not only did Jesus preach, but He also taught: "Then Jesus went about all the cities and villages, teaching in their synagogues, preaching the gospel of the kingdom, and healing every sickness and every disease among the people (Mt 9: 35)." And Jesus (His disciples in particular) also baptized those who accepted the gospel: "Therefore, when the Lord knew that the Pharisees had heard that Jesus made and baptized more disciples than John, though Jesus Himself did not baptize, but His disciples (John 4: 1, 2)." Many books have been written on how Jesus made disciples. However, one does not need to speculate. The Bible clearly indicated the process that the Master used to make disciples is the same He gave to His disciples in the Great Commission formula. (1) He preached, (2) He baptized, and (3) He taught.

Christ's Method of Teaching

In previous chapters, emphasis has already been put on preaching and baptizing. At this moment, we need to discover and emulate Christ's way of teaching His adherents to make them fully devoted disciples. Why did Christ choose twelve, and then seventy among His followers? We do not know. Why did Jesus give His final command to the then eleven only? We do not know. What we do know is that Christ is God and cannot err. He continued to meet with the crowd and spent time with them as well. He might, through His interaction with them, make evaluation of those with the potentiality to become disciples. He knew beforehand the hearts of the true prospective disciples. It is no secret that Jesus and the twelve had developed a deeper master-student friendship relationship. Jesus was intimately involved in the lives of the twelve. They ate together, prayed together, and always spent time together. Because of their closeness with the Master, it is obvious that they were better equipped for the work than any other ones. As such, they became not only disciples but also disciplers with the responsibility to train others to become disciple-makers. Today's church, the extension of the twelve, has the same mission to make disciples. How did Christ teach the twelve? What did He teach to them? If we are to fulfill the mandate of the Great Commission, we must emulate Christ's method of teaching. Not only do we need to follow Jesus' technique, but we must also teach what He was teaching.

Christ's methodology of teaching His disciples comprises of at least three elements. In other words, to become a graduate disciple at Christ's school, there were three requirements to satisfy. In addition to the general teaching class (crowd and disciples), the twelve were subject to: (1) Attending small group teaching, (2) training or mentorship, and (3) doing and turning in assignments (mission and service).

Requirement #1: Attending Small Group Class Teaching

In addition to the general teaching class where Jesus provides instructions for all His hearers, including His disciples, He specifically holds a small group teaching for the twelve. The Synoptic Gospels are filled with examples of Jesus simultaneously teaching both the crowd and His disciples (Mt 11: 1). If we are to follow Christ's method, the church should practice both corporate teaching for the congregation at large and small group teaching particularly for new converts. There are many instances where the Master gives specific instructions to His disciples only. For example, Luke reports that the disciples asked Jesus to teach them to pray. "Now it came to pass, as He was praying in a certain place, when He ceased, that one of His disciples said to Him, "Lord, teach us to pray, as John also taught his disciples" (Lk 11: 1)." Not only did Christ grant their request, but He also taught them to persevere in praying (11: 2-13). One of the key moments of Jesus offering a particular presentation to His disciples can be read in all the Synoptic Gospels (Mt 24: 1-14; Mk 13: 1-13; Lk 21: 5-19). Matthew gives hint that only the disciples attended this class. "Now, as He sat on the Mount of Olives, the disciples came to Him privately, saying, Tell us, when these things will be? And what will be the sign of Your coming, and of the end of the age? (Mt 24: 3)" Teaching is so vital that Jesus puts aside some quality time to instruct His disciples. There is no complete understanding of the Word without teaching.

Christ pursues the teaching ministry even after His resurrection. Indeed, it wasn't until He rose from the dead that the disciples possessed a better comprehension of Jesus' mission. They understood what He used to tell them about His sufferings, death, and resurrection. That teaching happened twice on the day of His resurrection after the Risen Savior met two of His disciples on the Emmaus Road and then the eleven hiding for fear of the Jews. He gave them a Bible study on the prophecies of the Bible concerning Him (Lk 24: 13-47). There cannot be understanding of Scriptures, growth, and maturity among new converts without teaching. Jesus' first disciples were ordinary people with no special education. Christ through teaching prepared and used them to bring the good news all over the places. Jesus sets the example: the early church practices it (Ac 2:42), the apostle Paul does it, and encourages his co-laborers to do the same. It is high time for the church to recognize that baptism is not the end of new converts' spiritual journey; it is just the beginning. Teaching is one of the core elements of discipleship. It sheds light on biblical truths and opens the eyes of the students of the Word. "And beginning at Moses and all the prophets, he expounded unto them in all the Scriptures the things concerning Himself. And their eyes were opened, and they knew him; and he vanished out of their sight (Lk 24: 27, 31)". Our role in making disciples is to properly teach the Scriptures and encourage new converts to search for themselves like the Jews of Berea (Ac 17: 11). Let us follow Christ's method of making disciples and teach what He taught.

What Did Christ Teach His Disciples?

Jesus does not leave His church in darkness in regard to what they are supposed to teach. We should not teach our wisdom or philosophy, not what the world wants to know but what they are supposed to know to become disciples. Jesus in His own words tells us what to preach, "teaching them to observe all things that I have commanded you (Mt 28: 20a)." The things that Jesus had commanded can be found in all the Gospels. It is no time for an exhaustive study; however, the Sermon on the Mount in the Gospel of Matthew (chapters 5-7) gives a panoramic view of Christian ethics which all new converts should be aware of. He taught them that things may go weary, but special blessings will be the reward of the faithful ones. Once they accept Him as Savior and Lord, they become part of God's family. As such, their behavior must be different from those who do not know him. The apostle Peter summarizes it as follows: "But you are a chosen generation, a royal priesthood, a holy nation, His own special people, that you may proclaim the praises of Him who called you out of darkness into His marvelous light; who once were not a people but are now the people of God, who had not obtained mercy but now have obtained mercy (1 Pt 2: 9, 10)." As God's people, they are the salt and the light of the world. Jesus taught His disciples to place their confidence in God, the Great Provider, who cares for them. He instructed them about God's law, which is the revelation of His loving character. They are supposed to obey and keep not the letter but rather the spirit of God's eternal law. Jesus taught His disciples self denial and humility, generosity and perseverance, interpersonal relations and respect for others, the golden rule…etc. Among many other Christian principles, and in addition to prayer, Jesus also taught his disciples the basic concept of God's kingdom, which is love. In other words, Matthew summarizes Christ's teachings as loving God and one's neighbor: "Jesus said to him, ""You shall love the LORD your God with all your heart, with all your soul, and with all your mind. This is the first and great commandment. And the second is like it: You shall love your neighbor as yourself"" (Mt 22: 37-39)."

Requirement #2: Attending Training and Mentorship class

Training was a fundamental element in Christ's teaching program for his disciples. It is practically impossible to make disciples without being one personally. The disciple generally reproduces what their master has taught or shown to them. A true disciple of Jesus is basically someone who makes the commitment to follow him and to do what Christ has done. This entails a process of practical learning, being on the spot to watch or observe attentively what the Master does. It is noteworthy to underline that the disciples paid great attention to Jesus in this field. Three of them (Peter, James, and John) were with Him most of the times. For example, when Jesus went to resurrect Jairus' daughter, he took them with him (Mk 5: 37). Being in a training session, they watched how the Master performed the miracle. He had put everybody except the parents and his disciples outside to act upon the miracle (Mk 5: 40, 41). The apostle Peter, one of the trainees, having seen what Jesus did, performed an analogous miracle reported in the book of Acts. He did exactly the same thing that Jesus had done. "But Peter put them all out, and knelt down and prayed. And turning to the body he said, "Tabitha, arise." And she opened her eyes, and when she saw Peter she sat up. Then he gave her his hand and lifted her up; and when he had called the saints and widows, he presented her alive (Ac 9: 40, 41)." The Bible is filled with parallel miracles where the disciples reproduced what Jesus had done. He healed a man with infirmity for 38 years (John 5: 5-9); Peter and John made an identical healing for a lame man (Ac 3: 2-9). In this same context, Peter performed another parallel miracle (Ac 9: 5, 6).

Not only did Jesus train His disciples but He also mentored them. Mentorship was part of Christ's syllabus. There are many times that the disciples could not catch Jesus' teaching. That generally happened when Christ taught the master class (crowd and disciples) in parables. They rarely asked any questions to Jesus when He preached or taught the crowd. However, when they got home, they privately asked their questions. In Luke 11, for instance, Jesus made a beautiful prayer. Amazed by this, the disciples in particular said to the Master to teach them to pray, which he did (Lk 11: 1-4). Matthew 13 is a turning point in Jesus' ministry. In this chapter, he begins talking in parables to reveal the mysteries of the kingdom of heavens. This form of speech appears to be unfamiliar to the disciples (Mt 13.10). While sitting by the seaside, a great crowd gathered around him. In verses 24-30, he tells them the parable of the tares. His disciples did not get the sense of that parable. However, when they got home, they came to him for explanation. Then Jesus sent the multitude away and went into the house. And His disciples came to Him, saying, "Explain to us the parable of the tares of the field (Mt 13: 36)." Through his mentoring session, Jesus always answers his disciples' questions, and this time again he explains to them the meaning of this parable (Mt 13: 37-43). Another example of Jesus mentoring his disciples is found in Matthew 17. While Peter, James, and John were with Christ on the Mount of Transfiguration, the remaining disciples were unable to cure a demon-possessed child brought to them (Mt 17: 16). However, when he rejoined them, he cast out the demon and healed the boy (17: 18). Then Jesus answered his disciples' questions and mentored to them how to perform such miracles. Then the disciples came to

Jesus privately and said, "Why could we not cast it out?" So Jesus said to them, "Because of your unbelief; for assuredly, I say to you, if you have faith as a mustard seed, you will say to this mountain, 'Move from here to there,' and it will move; and nothing will be impossible for you. However, this kind does not go out except by prayer and fasting (Mt 17: 19-21)."

Mentorship is an effective means of teaching, and a church needs to embrace it. While listening to Apollos' powerful preaching with some needed theological adjustment, Aquila and Pricilla took him with them and mentored him. "Now a certain Jew named Apollos, born at Alexandria, an eloquent man and mighty in the Scriptures, came to Ephesus. This man had been instructed in the way of the Lord; and being fervent in spirit, he spoke and taught accurately the things of the Lord, though he knew only the baptism of John. So he began to speak boldly in the synagogue. When Aquila and Priscilla heard him, they took him aside and explained to him the way of God more accurately (Ac 18: 24-26)." If we really want to transform our new converts from members to disciples, we must take time not only to teach them but also to mentor them. Do not criticize them; let us rather teach them the right way to do things.

Requirement #3: Doing and Turning In Assignments (Mission)

Discipleship is not a passive but an active vocabulary. A disciple is someone who accepts Christ as their personal Savior, commits to abiding in him and bearing fruit through the sharing of the good news of salvation. Once a person is trained and becomes a disciple, they must be at work. People are trained and mentored to become fruit-bearing disciples. Christ knows that very well. Though discipleship is a lifelong process, Jesus did not keep training and mentoring his disciples indefinitely without having them reach out the mission field. The Synoptic Gospels mention three specific assignments that Jesus gave his disciples as partial fulfillment of their discipleship program. In the first assignment, Jesus sent the twelve disciples two by two to preach the kingdom of God. Matthew gives a more detailed account of this evangelistic endeavor. Luke reports that they went where they were sent and performed a lot of healings. "So they departed and went through the towns, preaching the gospel and healing everywhere (Lk 9: 6)." Only Luke precisely gives a clear account of the second assignment (Lk 10: 1-24). At this time, seventy disciples were sent out to preach the gospel. They were also held accountable in this mission. Not only did they go, but they also provided the Master with a report (10: 17). Being satisfied with the results, Jesus told them to rejoice by the fact their names are written in heavens, and joyfully praised his Father (10: 20, 21). Mark and Matthew elaborated more on the third assignment; however, Matthew's account is the most used. This third assignment (Mt 28: 16-20; Mk 16: 15-21; Lk 24: 46-49; Jn 20: 20, 21) was given to the eleven being present at that time and to every converted believer. In other terms, Jesus' command to go and tell is required of everyone. Submission is one of the characteristics of a disciple. In all three assignments, the disciples obeyed Jesus' mandate. They went and the second time they brought a positive report. The eleven graduated about fifty days after Jesus' resurrection, on the Day of the Pentecost. What's about you, my friend? Do you also want to graduate from Christ's school of discipleship?

Can Today's Church Really Make Disciples?

We have discovered in previous and current chapters the technique used by Christ in making disciples. He evangelized the people and through his disciples baptized those who accepted the good news. He then taught them the principles of his kingdom with the duty of reproducing the work he had done. In simple terms, the Great Commissions can be summarized in two key assignments: (1) through intentional evangelism, seeking and bringing the lost in the front door, and (2) through discipleship, keeping and preventing them from going out the back door of the church. With the help of the Holy Spirit, the twenty-first century church can still make disciples. It is possible to transform new converts from simply church members to disciples by following what we have learned from Christ's way and method of making disciples. There is no variation in Christ. The Holy Spirit is still at work. We just have to contextualize and actualize the ways and methods that the Savior employed during the first century. Today's church needs to focus more on discipleship, which is an efficient way to motivate new converts to grow in their walk with Jesus. Discipleship must be the top priority and culture of the church. Jesus put emphasis on making disciples. Old church members must be taught and empowered to care for the new believers. We must teach the current members how to befriend new converts in incorporating them in church's friendship network. Making new converts become disciples is not simply the duty of the pastoral body; it is the responsibility of the whole body of Christ. This is a corporate work given to the entire church by Jesus Christ. In other terms, this work requires the involvement of the entire church family. For example, coaching them, sharing Bible texts with them, praying with and for them, teaching them good cooking habits, and supporting them in their growth process are different ways to disciple new converts.

Christ's way and method will always bring success. Let us follow them. Nurturing the newly baptized is very critical in their process of being disciples. The best way to nurture them is to tell and teach them how to maintain a personal, constant, and spiritual relationship with Christ. Like Jesus, we need to take ample time to pray for and with them, and teach them how to pray as well. Jesus' habit was to start His day with prayer (Mk 1:35). Do not assume that they already knew that. Encourage new converts to regularly attend the church services (He 10: 25); that was Jesus' custom (Lk 4: 16). One of the best ways for the neophytes to grow in Christ is to teach them to always read and study the Bible. The Scriptures testify about Jesus (Jn 5: 39). The Word of God is a weapon against the enemy (Mt 4: 4; Eph 6:10); it will preserve them from sinning (Ps 119: 11), and help them to walk in the light (Ps 119: 105). Creating an interesting and in-depth Bible study class for new converts will help them to experience this growth in the knowledge of Jesus Christ. As member of God's family, the new believer should be taught to live a holy life (Mt 5: 48) with the empowering of the Holy Spirit. Let them know that they will not be able to do that on their own (Jn 15: 5), but it is possible through Christ (Ph 4: 13). Another key factor that will help them progress in their spiritual journey is witnessing. Train them to present Christ in a way that people could put their trust in God. Conflicts can facilitate their growth in Jesus; do not tell them that they will be exempt of problems. Christ says they will have tribulations in the world (Jn 16: 33), but promises to be with them always (Mt 28: 20b).

One of the plausible ways for the church to make disciples is to build several retention ministries. Those ministries will facilitate their assimilation and involvement in church activities. We should not only tell new converts to minister, but we must also teach them how to do so. Have them accompany us while doing evangelistic and missionary work, such as the distribution of health literature or religious pamphlets, etc. Provide them with extra copies for their personal ministry. Enroll them in various ministries and pair them with experienced members. Do not hesitate to take them with you when giving a Bible study to a non believer. Train them to pray silently while learning attentively the way you study with the person. We can incorporate them by giving them a list of one or three church members to call. If we intentionally follow Christ's methods, we will conclude that making disciples is not as complicated as we might think. Even though we are living in a more secular society, transforming our new converts from members to disciples becomes even easier. Teach or show a new convert how to share some biblical truths with their peers through texting or emails is simple ways to make them disciples. What we need most today to make disciples is intentionality, submission to Christ, the anointing of the Holy Spirit, and patience.

Discipleship is not static but dynamic; therefore, we must be patient with new converts in the process of making them disciples. Christ's disciples were very slow, and the Savior was extremely patient with them (Peter, Philip, James, John, Judas, etc.). We should not expect them to change automatically, or quickly give up the old habits they have cherished for so long. Our biggest stumbling block in making disciples is that we forget that the One who gave the mandate has never failed His promise. He has promised to be with us, and He will always be. "And lo, I am with you always, even to the end of the age." Amen (Mt 28: 20b). Let us therefore follow Christ's command of making disciples and display an attitude of total obedience!

PRAGMATIC QUESTIONS

Q1: What should I do to become a disciple?

A1: Accept Jesus as your personal Savior by:

Responding positively to the invitation of those coming to share the gospel with you.

Being baptized in the name of the Father, Son, and Holy Spirit.

Attending a Bible study class for further instructions.

Being member of a community of faith that loves and obeys Jesus.

Developing new habits of living (devotion, prayer and Bible reading, fellowship).

Sharing your new faith with others.

Staying connected to Christ.

Q2: How can I help someone to become a disciple?

A2: Pray first and then:

Go and share the good news of salvation with them.

Persuade them to accept Jesus as their personal Savior and baptize them.

Teach them all that Christ has commanded you.

Encourage them to implement the points (d, e, f, and g) of A1.

You may start the process by simply inviting this person to church and also through good behavior and acts of kindness. Always remember that is the Holy Spirit who converts people. Whenever you even try to lead or introduce someone to Christ, you are on your way to making a disciple.

Q3: Can anyone become a disciple? In other words, if someone has gone astray after accepting Jesus, can they still be or become disciple?

A3: Regardless of someone's past, no matter what they have done, or regardless of where they have been, anyone can be or become a disciple. The best thing to do is to run to Jesus. A clear and convincing answer to that question can be found in the story of Peter, one of the most influential disciples. As a fisherman, Mark firstly recorded his acceptance of becoming a disciple (Mk 1:16-18). Later on, Matthew reported that three times he denied knowing Christ and being His disciple (Mt 26:69-75). However, despite Peter's denial, Christ did not give up on him. The apostle John, the last surviving disciple among the twelve, wrote about his restoration and reintegration in the discipleship ministry (Jn 21:15-19). Indeed, who can ignore Peter's great contribution to the Christian Church after Jesus reintegrated him as one simply reads the first fifteen chapters of the book of Acts? My friend, I am pleased to boldly tell you that there is a place for everyone in Christ's discipleship school, and that anyone can become a disciple.

Bible Reading: Mt 28: 19, 20; Jn 15: 1-16; 2 Co 5: 17; Mt 7: 21-27; Re 12: 17; 14: 12; He 10: 25

CHAPTER SEVEN
LITERATURE REVIEW

This chapter deals with the summary reviews of some critical books read for the programming and implementation of this project. Those writings have been tremendously helpful in getting materials for the preparation of this discipleship seminar. For instance, preparing the presentations, conducting research, and asking questions, etc, requires expertise. Therefore, it is useless to say that the launching of this discipleship program has required an extensive amount of reading and orderly research in order to get a better understanding of this crucial matter. This cram covers various topics, from self-discipline and spirituality to psychology, from evangelism to discipleship, from church growth to mentoring, nurturing, and retention. Considering the importance of leadership in the process of forming disciples, the literature reviewed has also included material on leadership.

Professional Development as Transformative Learning,
New Perspective for Teachers of Adults
By Patricia Cranton
Cranton points out that the traditional ways of adult and continuing education were based on experts who impress their ideas on learners without developing their personal advancement. For the purpose of this project, a thorough reading of chapters four, five, and six has been tremendously helpful. These three chapters can be viewed as the pivotal point of this book.

The author clearly shows how teachers and facilitators can and must be understood as adults engaged in transformative learning. After underlining the importance of self-directed learning, she puts great emphasis on critical reflection and its role in self-directed learning. More than anything, critical thinking holds the key for transformation in self-directed learning. She then argues that the combination of self-directed learning with critical thinking produces a transformative agent for both learner and educator. *Professional Development as Transformative Learning* provides the reader with practical and intellectual information.

Practical Psychology for Pastors
By William R. Miller and Kathleen A. Jackson

Dealing with new converts is not an easy endeavor for the setting of a Christ-based discipleship model. New converts mostly come from various backgrounds and have sometimes gone through several traumatisms. As such, it is fundamental for the sake of the project to get acquainted with literature relating to psychology. The way the authors depict practical issues on psychology, such as reflective listening, formulation of a problem, building a more resourceful community, and so on, plays a critical role in the task of teaching and counseling in the context of this project. The historical overview provides a good perspective for understanding one's own presuppositions. The chapter topics cover some of the most common problems a pastor will encounter in ministry.

The chapter on "Pastoral Self-Care," which offers advice on maintaining psychological health, avoiding crisis, and preventing personal and occupational burnout, has been utilized to assist the postulant disciples to be balanced and also take good care of their own being. Change has always been a great enemy. The reading of this practical manual conveys ways to help people build personal motivation for change. Practical Psychology for Pastors provides what pastoral leaders can learn from psychology that will assist them in ministry.

How People Grow: What the Bible Reveals about Personal Growth
By Dr. Henry Cloud and Dr. John Townsend

Discipleship is not a stagnant but a dynamic and lifetime process. It therefore requires personal growth in various domains such as the emotional, cognitive, and spiritual. That is in fact the core of this project, moving new converts from members to disciples. The authors of this book, Drs Cloud and Townsend, put great emphasis on the importance of spiritual growth. They also proposed, from a biblical viewpoint, some useful tools to help people realizing their dependence on God to solve their conflicts and enhance their relationships with others in order to attain that growth. The chapters about God's grace, the growth in forgiveness, and the pain of guilt, project sound resonance to an attentive reader. The work is full of great stories of real people, which is one of the most valuable pieces of it.

The authors discuss several essential processes that make people grow. They also explain how those processes fit into a biblical understanding of spiritual growth and theology. Not only do they underline the responsibilities of pastors, counselors, and others who assist in the growth process, but they also echo the role that people must play in their personal growth. The helpful and practical questions found at the end of each chapter allow the conclusion that there is something for everyone in this book, especially for those who desire personal growth and for people who are in a position to guide others in their own growth.

The Call: Finding and Fulfilling The Central Purpose of Your Life
By Os Guinness

New converts need to know that their allegiance to Christ implies three important aspects of the spiritual journey: the call, the commission, and the contribution. In his book, *The Call*, Os Guinness examines the biblical mandate to surrender ourselves to God's call in all aspects of life. The author approaches his subject with the understanding that all Christians are called by God to serve Him and the body in some special way. He uses several convincing stories to show how people in Christianity or outside have answered a call in their lives, found meaning, purpose, and joy, and left their incredible mark on history.

After a thorough reading of this manual, the following considerations can be made. It becomes easy to discover that one must be devoted to Jesus instead of their service to Jesus. Christ's follower ought to be inner-directed by God rather than other-directed by the opinions of others. God calls us to a life of faith, we need to spend deliberate quality time with Him and glorify Him in every detail of life. This book has been helpful in the preparation of material for this project. Once people know why they are called they get motivated to live in harmony with their call.

The Evangelistic Love of God and Neighbor:
A Theology of Witness and Discipleship
By Scott J. Jones

One of the essential reasons we fail in making disciples resides in the fact that we attempt to create a separation between evangelism and discipleship. In his book, *The Evangelistic Love of God*, Jones provides convincing arguments to close this gulf. He sees evangelism as initiation into Christian discipleship. Throughout this manual, he argues that evangelism is best understood as an aspect of the church's mission that seeks to help persons enter into Christian discipleship.[1] Evangelism is therefore seen as the proclamation of the Word of God. The best way to positively respond to that proclamation is to become a disciple in living an obedient life to God's will by making other disciples.

The centrality of God's saving love for humankind leads to the coming of Christ and the proclamation of the reign of God. When we love God, we obey Him by becoming active agents of the kingdom. As obedient disciples, we witness and proclaim the good news to fellow human beings. The author also underlines that the ministry of evangelism is both motivated and governed by the love that Christ commanded. The goal of discipleship is to bring Christian maturity.

The Cost of Discipleship
By Dietrich Bonhoeffer

Following Jesus should not be a blinded decision; in other words, being a disciple is not an easy task and requires much from the adherent. At this level, it appears very logical for new converts to know what their decision entails. In his book, *The Cost of Discipleship*, Dietrich Bonhoeffer clearly explains what it means to be Jesus' disciple. In other words, the book's major theme centers on what it really means to be a disciple of Christ. As per the author, Christ calls us to come and die. Christ wants all of us; nothing is to be held back. One is either a disciple of Christ, or they are not; there is no middle ground.

Choosing to be a disciple of Christ is to be exposed to rejection because Christ, Himself, was rejected. Being a disciple of Christ is to accept sufferings.

Following Jesus Christ's steps is to concur to face all the calamities and mistreatment that He had to go through. Therefore, as disciples of Christ, we must take up our cross, not just any cross, but the one Jesus has provided for each one of us, and we are to carry it until the end. The author clearly differentiates what he calls cheap grace and costly grace, and also conveys the true meaning of discipleship.

No Man Left Behind: How to Build and Sustain a Thriving, Disciple-Making Ministry for every Man in your Church
By Patrick Morley

The writer of any gender-inclusive project, after reading this book, will be tempted to change its title from *No Man Left Behind* to *Nobody (Man or Woman) Left Behind*. This has been an exemplary case for the topic understudy. This book is a great resource for men's ministry and an inspiration to keep it on track. The authors suggest that the best way to start this program is to create a vision for the men stating where one wants to take them, find a way to help others to catch that vision, and develop a mechanism for them to keep the momentum. In other words, the book clearly lays out the psychology of how to do it, the psychology of the process, the system, and how to implement it.

The chapter on discipleship, full of biblical passages to back up what has been said, constitutes an invaluable resource for the development of a discipleship program. And when that program is properly implemented, it will produce committed disciples, dynamic leaders, and a productive church environment. The techniques suggested by the authors to develop a thriving men's ministry program are applicable to any discipleship program including men and women. They give great ideas on how to transform new church members to become disciples.

Understanding Your Potential: Discovering the Hidden You
By Myles Munroe

New believers generally think that, because of their lack of maturity in faith, they are unqualified to do anything good in the ecclesiological realm. However, Dr. Myles Munroe in his book *Understanding Your Potential* points out their wrongness. The reading of this book instills the conviction that every new convert has the ability to do something great and important as soon as they develop a relationship with Christ. In fact, the author believes that human beings were endowed with certain potentials at birth, which they need to tap into.

This manual is a motivating factor that can lead someone to discover the awesome potential trapped with them. The author illustrates his point by using the biblical scenario of Joshua, the successor of Moses, where the Lord told him to be courageous for he already had what he needed to get the job done. Whoever reads this book will feel uncomfortable with their present state of accomplishment and make plans to further their achievements in life.

How To Ask Great Questions:
Guide Your Group to Discovery With These Proven Techniques
By Karen Lee —-Thorp

The development of a discipleship program for new converts necessitates a lot of communication skills. Asking good questions, due to its importance, should be considered as an art, a science, and could not be a dull and boring activity. It requires psychological, technical, and philosophical approaches. In her book, *How to ask Questions*, Lee—-Thorp goes along with this understanding when she presents the top ten principles for asking great questions. The volume seems small, but it is very profound.

From the very beginning, the author sets the purpose and tells what the book is about, which is the power of a good question. It is in fact a crucial point, since we will have to interact with people. Many times, people just ask questions, but after reading this book, one can find the fundamental reasons of questioning: who, what, when, where, why, and how? A question which is asked inappropriately may have a negative impact on an individual or a group of people. Therefore, it is very important to learn how to ask proper and accurate questions. With emphasis on some moral key issues such as honesty, and truth, which give the book a positive image, the writer teaches respectful behavior in regard to how ask questions in order not to discomfit others. The principles discussed in this book have been helpful to the realization of the project.

Organic Disciplemaking:
Mentoring Others Into Spiritual Maturity and Leadership
By Dennis McCallum and Jessica Lowery

The development of a discipleship program for new converts necessitates having mentorship skills for a successful implementation. In their book *Organic Disciplemaking*, McCallum and Lowery share a great deal of information on how to mentor others into spiritual maturity. They give a broader view of discipleship by pointing out that discipleship does not stop at the point of established faith. Rather, discipleship is a long-term process and should continue until a person (new convert) is able to pass on to others what they have learned.

The authors accomplish a skillful work in providing in this manual the basics needed to mentor someone into spiritual maturity and leadership. Several critical principles for growth are found in this book. More importantly, the writers show that discipleship is a dynamic process. One of the key reasons for coaching or mentoring a disciple is for them to become disciple-makers. The reading of this book has been very helpful in the sense that it provides various practical ideas and insights for the development of a discipleship program for new converts.

Becoming a Healthy Disciple: Ten Traits of a Vital Christian
By Stephen A. Macchia

A disciple is someone who tries to live like Jesus and produces good fruit for the everlasting kingdom. To be able to bear fruit, the disciple must be healthy. In other words, they are to develop and maintain a good relationship with the Lord Jesus Christ. In his foundational and practical book *Becoming A Healthy Disciple*, Macchia unfolds the secrets to a vital Christian life. He also asks the direct and challenging questions that every individual needs to answer in their daily attempt to emulate Christ.

In the very beginning of the book, the author clearly explains what a healthy disciple is and shows that discipleship is a continuous state of learning from the Master, Jesus Christ. His thought is fully summarized in the following statement:

> Becoming a healthy disciple is a lifelong journey. We won't ever arrive at the fullest picture of what God requires of us. Discipleship is apprenticeship, and the Master doesn't expect perfection, only skill development that leads to a deeper relationship along the way. We will fall short of his glory, and we will disappoint him more often than we care to imagine. But the fact is, the awesome love of the Lord for all his disciples –

past, present, and future – is unfathomable, unconditional, indestructible, and incredible. Living by human ability and insight, we will disappoint him, but when we live by his strength and provision, we delight him and bring him great joy.[2]

As they are called to a new life in Christ, this practical book on Christian discipleship is capable of teaching new converts how they shall live to emulate Christ and become a healthy disciple. This manual has been a tremendous tool in the preparation of the materials for this project.

Becoming A Fruit-Bearing Disciple
By Terry Thomas

Bearing fruit is the core assignment that Jesus gave to his disciples. It is not optional but mandatory. In his book, *Becoming A Fruit-Bearing Disciple*, Terry Thomas appears to catch very well this requirement of Jesus. He raises the critical concern of how to biblically mature new converts in the faith in order to bring fruit for the heavenly kingdom. The author outlines and defines in practical ways the process of how one becomes a fruit-bearing disciple. He cites his own congregation as a proving example to establish a process to develop mature disciples.

The key technique as per the writer for someone to become a fruit-bearing disciple is to hang with the Master. At this level, one can learn Jesus' process or approach to make disciples. In other words, when we hang with Jesus, we will learn all the lessons that can help us to make followers. To be disciple makers like Jesus, one must learn how to mingle with those who do not know Christ and meet their needs. Finally, to develop fruit-bearing disciples, the writer compels intentional training. As per Thomas, discipleship is costly. However, he refers to the beatitudes in the Sermon on the Mount as compensation and the joys of a disciple.

Growing True Disciples:
New Strategies for Producing Genuine Followers of Christ
By George Barna

New converts are considered babes in faith. They need to be nurtured in order to become true disciples. In his book *Growing True Disciples*, George Barna proposes several strategies for producing genuine followers of Christ. He begins the book with the need of this writing and the necessity to focus on disciple making within the church. He also describes what scriptural discipleship is and how it is much more than accomplishing a few things for God. The author gives an extended view of discipleship, which is devoting one's whole self to God and the teachings of Christ. Not only does he discuss the importance of discipleship, but he also gives a concise look at discipleship exemplified in the Bible.

This book constitutes an invaluable resource for the realization of this project, which is transforming new converts from members to disciples. The author clarifies that the ultimate goal of a disciple is to become more like Jesus. The reading of this manual provides some significant resource that can lead to the development and implementation of a Christ-based discipleship model within the church.

Christ's Way of Making Disciples
By Philip G. Samaan

Making disciples for Christ is not a somewhat easy effort. Discipline and methodology are critical for the accomplishment of this task. We cannot offer what we do not have. In other words, one needs to be a disciple first before being able to make disciples. In his book *Christ's Way of Making Disciples*, Philip G. Samaan shows how Christ did make disciples. In this manual, the author emphasizes that the need of the church today is not merely to make members, but rather to make disciples. The writer explores the dynamic process and progressive steps of Christ's strategies in making disciples. He also demonstrates how Jesus transformed the lives of many people to make them fruit-bearing disciples.

The author does not simply underline the necessity for the church to make disciples, but he also enumerates several characteristics of a true disciple. For instance, a true disciple is someone who lives for the supreme purpose of glorifying God in producing good fruit for the eternal kingdom. In summary, the nine characteristics of a true disciple that the writer cites in this book have been a source of great inspiration in the preparatory work of this project.

Making Disciples: Developing Lifelong Followers of Jesus
By Ralph Moore
As one considers the core message of the Great Commission, making disciples can be seen as everybody's business. In other terms, those who call themselves Christians or disciples of Christ have the duty of making disciples. In this manual, the author's genius for realness and simplicity makes any authentic believer want to go and make disciples as soon as they accept Jesus as their personal Savior. He shares great stories and gives insight for building disciple-making churches that reproduce and change people's lives. One of the main lessons drawn from the reading of this book is the emphasis put on intentional discipleship and the possibility to get every individual to embark in this marvelous ministry.

As per Moore, "there is no mystery involved in the process of making disciples. You only need a love for people and a sense of responsibility toward the Lord and His command to "make disciples of all nations" (Mt 28:19)."[3]

Finding Them, Keeping Them:
Effective Strategies for Evangelism and Assimilation in the Local Church
By Gary McIntosh & Glen Martin
A church must be intentional in doing evangelism if they want to keep the neophytes. In their book *Finding Them, Keeping Them*, McIntosh and Martin propose ten key strategies that really go along with Jesus' command found in Matthew 28:19. The first five strategies are about how to do practical evangelism. However, it is worth underlining that the last two principles convey a clear message with the comprehension that evangelism is a dynamic activity. These two strategies, progression evangelism and production evangelism, lead to the second part of the book, which is about assimilation or retention of new converts.

In the second segment of the book, the authors mention five techniques and strategies to assimilate new converts in the life of the church so they can become disciple-makers. If the strategies cited in this work are contextually applied, they will definitely help keep new converts in the church. The reading of this manual has played a critical role in finding methods to lead people to Christ and to keep them as they mature in their relationship with the risen Savior.

Values-Driven Leadership:
Discovering and DevelopingYour Core Values for Ministry
By Aubrey Malphurs

The call to make disciples seems nowadays to be no longer a priority. A church that wants to develop a Christ-based discipleship model must have a set of core values that will clearly define its priority. The new members need direction. They are searching for leadership to provide them with direction. In his book, *Values-Driven Leadership*, Malphurs offers crucial insights on the importance of core values and leadership. According to the author, "values enhance credible leadership. A church's core values are a vital part of its character, which is also determined by its mission, vision, and strategy."[4] Once the purpose is given, the new member will be motivated in order to accomplish it.

The author encourages preaching, teaching, and training to show that the special gifts found in Ephesians 4: 11 do not belong only to some specific categories but to all believers. This view is well expressed when he writes that a core value in many new paradigm churches is lay ministry. The value slogan is, "Every member a minister."[5] The training can be used to further implement the values. The writer stresses that pastors and leadership teams need to teach these values and help the members to catch them. The reading of this book provides good insights for the development and implementation of a Christ-based discipleship model for new converts.

The 21 Indispensable Qualities of a Leader:
Becoming the PersonOthers Will Want to Follow
By John C. Maxwell

Developing a successful discipleship program requires a lot of leadership skills. In fact, making disciples is an incontestable leadership endeavor. In this book, Maxwell teaches the qualities that one needs to be a leader and how to become a trustworthy leader. He also stresses the importance of leadership when he attempts to explain the failures of some people because of their lack of leadership. As per Maxwell, everything rises or falls on leadership. This manual describes the characteristics that leaders must possess and cultivate in order to be successful.

Though these twenty-one qualities are irrefutable for a leader to be successful, Maxwell puts a particular emphasis on character as one of the most important. The reading of this book helps not only to discover the qualities of a leader but also shows how to implement them. This manual has been tremendously useful in the preparation of this project.

1: Scott J. Jones, *The Evangelistic Love of God and Neighbor* (Nashville, TN: Abingdon Press, 2003), 65.

2: Stephen A. Macchia, *Becoming A Healthy Disciple: Ten Traits of a Vital Christian,* (Grand Rapids, MI: Baker Books, 2004), 14.

3: Ralph Moore, *Making Disciples: Developing Lifelong Followers of Jesus* (Ventura, CA: Regal, 2010), 17.

4: Aubrey Malphurs, *Values-Driven Leadership: Discovering and Developing Your Core Values for Ministry* (Grand Rapids, MI: Baker Books, 2004), 10.

5: Aubrey Malphurs, *Values-Driven Leadership: Discovering and Developing Your Core Values for Ministry* (Grand Rapids, MI: Baker Books, 2004), 124.

CHAPTER EIGHT
METHODOLOGY: FROM MEMBERS TO DISCIPLES

This discipleship program is designed to make new converts involve in church activities as soon as they accept Christ as their personal Savior. Personal observation and continuous complaints of church leaders about the non-participation of the newly baptized in the church's life have inspired this endeavor. This non-involvement is mostly caused by the lack of maturity in Christian affairs and a poor knowledge in their relationship with Christ. The problem being identified, a plan of action through a discipleship strategy was put in place in order to assimilate new converts in the life of the church. The vision has been communicated to the church and overwhelmingly accepted by the members. This program was to provide opportunities to the new believers to develop ministry skills. Provision was also made for the training of some ministry leaders before the launching of the project. After evaluation and necessary adjustments, a date has been set to start the discipleship program (see chapter ten).

Problem Statement
The church under study has been facing the challenge of simply making members for years. The church has failed to assimilate those who have been evangelized. The church too often equates baptism of new converts to the end of their spiritual journey, and overlooks Jesus' command of making disciples. As a result, the percentage of new converts leaving the church shortly after baptism due to lack of Christian maturity is considerably high (over 70%). The

non-involvement of new converts in church activities due to lack of maturity in their relationship with Christ has created the necessity for a Christ-based discipleship program that is biblically rooted, historically sound, and theologically relevant for new converts in this congregation.

Hypothesis

If that Church embraces this Christ-based discipleship program, new converts, shortly after their baptism, will know that they are committed to Christ. They will be able to establish the difference between church membership and discipleship. As a result, through solid biblical teaching, they will be confident and knowledgeable of church matters and become involved in different ministries. After the implementation of this program, the expectation was to see a great percentage of new converts getting involved in church activities and witnessing for the Lord. It is worth mentioning that new converts are not the only ones that refuse their collaboration. Their positive and joyful participation might constitute an incentive for the church at large that will move them from simply church members to committed disciples.

Objectives

The main objective of this initiative is to help new converts to become active participants in the church's life right after their baptisms and so on. In other terms, this project aims at enhancing the participation of new converts at a substantial percentage in the ministries of the church so they can become effective disciples. Jesus' mandate is to make disciples. "When a person becomes a Christian, the most basic need is no longer food, or water or shelter. The most basic need becomes the commitment to follow Christ; to be a disciple."[1]

The purpose of this endeavor is to develop a Christ-based discipleship model that can help every new convert build a good, constant, personal, and spiritual relationship with Jesus. If Christ's assignment found in Mathew 28: 19 is well understood and put into application, there is no doubt that the discipleship process begins with the teaching of the neophytes. In addition to the teaching aspect, the other components of a discipleship model, such as the study of the Word of God, the fellowship and fraternal communion, and mission will give new converts great insights of how to remain committed to Christ in order to live a life of service.

Research Design

The context of this project was the selected church under study. The participation of new converts in the church's life is mostly insignificant. This non-involvement in church activities due to a lack of maturity in their relationship with Christ leads most of the times to their leaving a few months after baptism. The objective of this project is to teach them how to grow in their relation with Christ, and become active participants of the church's establishment in the process of reaching the lost for God's kingdom.

Research Instruments

For the implementation of the project, information and data were gathered at the selected church by different methods, such as personal observation, questionnaires, pastoral visits, and surveys. A qualitative research method was used for data collection to design, implement, and evaluate the project. A pre- and post-test in the form of a questionnaire was administered to each participant at the beginning and end of the project. "Qualitative researchers tend to collect data in the field at the site where participants experience the issue or problem under study. They do not bring individuals to a lab, nor do they typically send out instruments for individuals to complete."[2] Having identified the discipleship needs of new converts, a set of spiritual disciplines has been determined to form the foundation for the Christ-centered discipleship program. These spiritual disciplines are developed in chapters five, ten, and eleven in particular.

Data Triangulation

To establish the validity of the qualitative research method utilized in this project, a data triangulation approach was adopted. Three different sources of collected data were considered, a survey (questionnaire), a 700-word essay from ten active participants, and face-to-face interviews with eight active participants. Five categories and coding were used, Loving (L), Understanding (U), Ministering (M), Equipping (E), and Networking (N). Data triangulation involves the use of different sources of data/information. A key strategy is to categorize each group or type of stakeholders for the program that is being evaluated.

The project consisted of ten two-hour sessions and was conducted at the church chosen:

- Pre-test and General Introduction on Discipleship,
- Theoretical Foundation of Discipleship
- Christ and Discipleship,
- The Holy Spirit and Discipleship,
- God's Word and Discipleship,
- Salvation and Discipleship,
- Prayer and Discipleship,
- Church and Discipleship,
- Stewardship and Discipleship, and
- Project Review and Post-test.

These modules were presented on the ladder of three basic characteristics of discipleship, which are Teaching, Mentoring (Coaching), and Witnessing. Each presentation followed a simple format (See Appendix C). The first thirty minutes were reserved for devotion (singing, reading of a short biblical passage, and praying) and a quick review of the material previously studied. Forty-five minutes were allotted to the introduction, and development of the new topic, twenty minutes for group discussion, and fifteen minutes for questions. Finally, ten minutes were set aside for conclusion and summary, and closing prayer. A theme song was chosen in the opening day by the participants.

The Participants
"The idea behind qualitative research is to purposefully select participants or sites that will best help the researcher understand the problem and the research question. This does not necessarily suggest random sampling or selection of a large number of participants and sites, as typically found in quantitative research."[3] There were two types of participants in this program. The targeted group (active participants) was selected among new converts, those who were baptized in the prior eighteen months. On December 6 and 7 of 2013, a special program was organized and prepared for about 39 new converts. Their participation was tremendous, and 32 of them registered for the discipleship seminar. The age group varied from 15 to 52 years including men and women. The second group of participants (adherent) included nine ministry leaders in the church. These church officers were not chosen randomly; they had been

trained to fulfill an important task throughout the project implementation. Their role was to make possible the involvement of new converts in the church activities. Nine small group panel discussions were formed in order to facilitate a one-on-one participation. Each small group panel discussion contained two new converts and a ministry leader serving as the group leader or mentor. These group leaders were also to train and disciple these new believers who should afterwards be able to evangelize, disciple, and train others in the same way. The main goal was "Transforming New Converts from Church Members to Disciples of Christ."

Measurement

The participation of new converts in church affairs has served as a measurement tool for evaluating the project. The ministry leaders were responsible for providing opportunities for the people group targeted in order to develop their ministry skills and enhance their participation in the program and the church at large. In-session participation was conducted by the facilitator during the seminar.

The mentors (Ministry Leaders) were provided with a report in regard to the new convert's involvement in ministries.

A 700-word essay was collected from ten active participants, and eight face-to-face interviews were conducted in lieu of the 700-word essay because these participants were unable to write.

The same information was requested for both means of collection. Both essay writers and interviewees had to express/answer the seven same ideas/questions concerning the following:

- The topics studied
- The meaning of love for a disciple
- The importance of studying the Word of God
- Their intent to minister to others
- Their willingness for continuous training
- Their eagerness to become a disciple
- Their comments and suggestions

Questions 2-5 were used for triangulation purposes; one and six for evaluation reason; and seven for possible means of improvement in the curriculum.

1: Jane Thayer, *Teaching for Discipleship: Strategies for Transformational Learning* (Unpublished, 2009), 4.

2: John W. Creswell, *Research Design: Qualitative, Quantitative, and Mixed Methods Approaches*, 3rd ed. (Los Angeles, CA: SAGE, 2009), 175.

3: John W. Creswell, *Research Design: Qualitative, Quantitative, and Mixed Methods Approaches*, 3rd ed. (Los Angeles, CA: SAGE, 2009), 178

CHAPTER NINE
PREPARATORY WORKS
FOR A DISCIPLESHIP PROGRAM

As already seen in preceding chapters, making disciples requires intentionality, extensive work, and careful preparation. Establishing of ministries that are pathways to the church has been pivotal for the discipleship program illustrated in chapter ten. It was a long-term initiative prior to our evangelistic series. In addition to spiritual activities, the church offers services to its members and to the community at large. In the summer of 2007, the church inaugurated a food pantry where they serve about eighty-six families twice a month. Once a month, they hold a soup kitchen ministry as they feed over one hundred people. Twice a year, the church offers a health fair to the community, which greatly attracts elderly people. Basic courses, including English as a second language (ESL) and computer literacy classes, are freely taught in the church facility. In regard to social activities, the church organizes each year two barbecues mostly attended by the youth on Memorial and Labor Days. It also holds on Labor Day a special program entitled "Back 2 School" during which school supplies are given to the parents. One of the most attended social activities, called Recreation Night, is organized at the end of each trimester with a significant presence of most youths from all denominations.

The church is also well-known in the community for providing other services such as weddings, children's presentations, and funerals for non-members who do not have any religious affiliation. At the end of each quarter (trimester), the church organizes a Friendship Day, also called Neighbor Day, on behalf of the surrounding neighborhood. The main purpose of this activity is to mingle with members of the community, know them better in order to identify their needs, and make plans to meet those needs. The church through these services becomes the church of the community.

In addition to the pathway ministries to the church, several other initiatives, such as a daily quarterly study online and a simple Bible study for new converts, have been taking place in the church. Moreover, prior to the launching of this project, the congregation intentionally put great emphasis on four other fundamental activities that are tremendously helpful in the realization of a Christ-centered discipleship program. These four activities put in place for the preparation of the discipleship program presented in chapter ten are: (1) Preparing the church, (2) Conducting a mentoring class for ministry leaders, (3) Doing a spiritual gifts assessment for new converts, and (4) Building retention ministries in the church. In addition to all evangelism strategies and good initiatives of discipleship, these techniques will easily help to plug new converts into small groups and ministries of the congregation.

Activity #1: Preparation of the Church

Several churches do not seem to be intentional in welcoming and incorporating new converts in their midst. Some old members leave no door open for the neophytes. Others expect and insist that new believers must upon their arrival meet their personal standards. It is therefore the responsibility of the pastoral body to prepare their congregation in receiving the newcomers. Church members need to understand that they have a moral obligation to welcome and assimilate new converts in the Body of Christ. If they are not trained to change their behavior, they may turn down and push away those whom the Lord has brought into his church. For example, before launching the Christ-based discipleship program found in chapter ten, various activities are set to prepare the church. A support group with the main goal of welcoming and befriending the newly baptized was created for new converts. A special training class on how to deal with the new believers was conducted for the old members. Six sermons on love, the importance for Christians to bear fruit, and human relationships were preached consecutively to the entire body. To complete the church's preparation, a weekend seminar on discipleship was presented; it was the starting point in the mentality change and the embracing of discipleship as a new culture in the church. There certainly are innumerable activities that can be done to prepare the church to receive new converts. Only a few suggestions are given in this segment; however, the bottom line is that the church must be prepared to welcome and assimilate new converts.

Activity #2: Mentoring Class

In this chapter, mentoring should be seen as a deliberate method and process employed to assist new converts in their Christian maturity. Prior to beginning a disciple program (see chapter ten), a formal mentoring class must be conducted for church officers at large, and for ministry leaders in particular. Mentoring the ministry leaders at first is very important in the process of making disciples. They are the ones in charge of guiding, advising, assimilating, and encouraging new converts. As such, they need to well comprehend the concept and be able to act properly. Mentors get to be patient while helping others to understand that being a disciple is a lifelong process. One must learn to better serve. If our old members and ministry leaders are not trained and mentored properly, they will be unable to mentor new converts. When ministry leaders are mentored in advance, the discipleship program will bring much success. Mentored ministry leaders play a critical role in transforming new converts from members to disciples. That is really an effective way to retain the neophytes and make lifelong disciples for Christ. It is time for the church to apply Christ's method. The Savior spent a significant amount of time to mentor His disciples; we must do as Christ did, mentoring others to become mentors as well.

Activity #3: Spiritual Gifts Assessment

One of the best ways to have a successful discipleship program for new converts is to get them involved in church ministries. However, this involvement becomes more practical when they are assimilated in areas where they are gifted. In other terms, it is crucial to involve the new believers in the areas where they can perform very well. They generally get embarrassed when they are asked to do something with which they are unfamiliar. A new female convert leaves her church just because she was asked to pray in public about one week of her baptism. One of the most important things to do before engaging new converts in church affairs is to determine or identify their talents through a spiritual gifts assessment. Each individual has been given at least one gift according to the apostle Paul. Some biblical scholars advance that there are between twenty and thirty spiritual gifts. The pastoral leadership under the influence of the Holy Spirit should be able to identify those gifts as new believers are being integrated in small groups and church retention ministries. Discovering these gifts before the launching of a discipleship program is tremendously helpful. As you will see in chapter ten, this program consists of different panel groups of discussion. The pre-identification of the spiritual gifts of the neophytes will help to plug new converts in appropriate, familiar, and comfortable ministries. They will be under the supervision of the right people to help them grow spiritually. This will also facilitate group evaluations.

Spiritual gifts assessment should be done for all members. Ministries become more effective and members more efficient in their performances. When spiritual gifts are actively functioning in the local congregation, God's grace abounds, human lives are positively affected, and God is glorified. The main purpose of the spiritual gifts is to praise God and build up the body of Christ. The apostle Paul depicts clearly the reasons why Christ gives spiritual gifts to his church: "And He Himself gave some to be apostles, some prophets, some evangelists, and some pastors and teachers, for the equipping of the saints for the work of ministry, for the edifying of the body of Christ (Eph 4: 11, 12)." Making disciples requires that new believers be empowered to exercise their God-given spiritual gifts in the local church to bring unity and harmony. When talents are transformed into spiritual gifts, they form models of ministries to serve the needs of the people and honor God.

Activity #4: Building Retention Ministries or Services

A church that is intentional in keeping new converts must show seriousness in involving them through small groups and retention ministries. These ministries must be established or reinforced prior to the new believers' arrival. They should not begin with new converts. These small groups must be functioning as they help the church to do the will of God. It becomes much easier to assimilate or incorporate the new believers in the church's life. One of the great advantages of the retention ministries is the fact that the setting is not complicated. Involvement or participation can be done through visitation ministries (hospitals, nursing homes, and prisons). Those groups include prayer ministry, literature distribution, usher, healthy cooking. These ministries also comprise Bible study, Bible reading, youth ministry, and choir. Getting these groups functioning in parallel with the discipleship program is beneficial and allows for short-term evaluations. There is a ministry available for the neophyte to involve, and the ministry leader at the same time can better supervise and mentor them. If the church sets all these services or ministries in advance, it becomes difficult for new converts to find excuses not to involve or walk away.

Once implemented, these four elements can be viewed as groundwork for the setting of a successful Christ-based discipleship program. When the church understands its mission, they will not wait to welcome but will invite others to join Christ's body. As they follow Christ's method of making disciples, church members will volunteer to be trained in order to mentor the newcomers through various ministries and/or services. Commenting on the importance of identifying spiritual gifts, a colleague of mine (Dr. Mary S. Minor, D.Min.) gives the following testimonial, which almost summarizes these four activities:

"She said, in 2012, a church member invited his neighbor to church. When the man's neighbor arrived at the church, he noticed that the physical church building was in desperate need of some repairs. A leaky roof caused water damage to some areas of the ceiling. He inquired about performing the repairs at a nominal labor cost. The Board of Trustees contracted his services. During the time he worked at the church, his truck broke down. He asked for permission to park his truck in the church parking lot. The man had recently become homeless and was sleeping in his truck. When the neighbors discovered the man's living conditions, they called the police and reported a homeless man sleeping in his vehicle in the church parking lot. The trustees invited him to sleep in the church while he completed the repairs to the church. He was among the twenty-six persons who completed a spiritual gifts assessment. His results indicated that he was equipped with the spiritual gifts of missionary, wisdom, faith, knowledge, exhortation, and administration. He is now a member of the congregation, and a member of the Board of Trustees, and he is the church's handyman. Some of the congregants contract him to do repairs on their homes. He was a tremendous help to my pastoral ministry and personal affairs."

Then, my friend said, "On November 3, 2013, my mother passed away. Her house required some repairs before it could be placed on the real estate market. This man was instrumental in performing and overseeing the repairs to the house. He used his administrative skills to plan and price out the job; he determined what materials were needed and worked within the prescribed budget. He offered to take on my nineteen-year-old nephew as his apprentice. He trained him to patch and repair drywall, paint walls, and match texture. My nephew took his newly acquired skills and painted some interior rooms at his parent's home. He was paid for his services and was allowed to live in the house rent-free until it is sold." My friend concludes her testimony saying, "A gift opens doors; it gives access to the great."

A church that does not identify the spiritual gifts of the members will ignore the potentiality of its human resources. Once their gifts are discovered, members should be put to work. That will give them a sense of belonging, and they will be more inclined to set their talents at the service of the Master and the congregation. Not only does their involvement keep them in church, but it can also benefit the body financially. It is the responsibility of the church to help the new convert discover and use the spiritual gift that the Holy Spirit has given them for the common good of Christ's body. When the process is properly done, the new member is being satisfied for their involvement in the church's affairs. Quoting George Barna, as they mention the importance of the spiritual gift, McIntosh and Martin write, "Unless you become involved in the activities of your church, you will never truly feel satisfied with that church."[1] The church can be more efficient in fulfilling its task when people get involved. Every baptized individual has at least received a gift from God. Nobody has received all the gifts. All the gifts are equally important, although some may be or appear greater than others. All the gifts are given to glorify God and edify the body of Christ in equipping the saints for ministry. It is therefore time to remember that every member has a role to play in the church. It is also critical to teach and help each new member to optimally use the gift that they have received from the Lord.

1:    Gary McIntosh & Glen Martin, *Finding Them, Keeping Them: Effective Strategies for Evangelism and Assimilation in the Local Church* (Nashville, TN: Publishing Group, 1992), 89.

CHAPTER TEN
THE FIELD WORK:
A TEN-SESSION DISCIPLESHIP PROGRAM

The main focus of this document is to transform new converts from simply church members to disciples of Christ as stated by the Savior in the Great Commission. Generally, most new converts leave the church shortly after their entrance, due to lack of maturity in church affairs and knowledge of Christ. Because they are not trained to get involved in the life of the congregation, their participation becomes very rare. When they are not solicited to exercise their talents and/or God-given gifts, they feel alienated and abandon the church. Leaving the church quickly after baptism is a real issue for the neophytes and a challenge for the church as well. We have been talking about it for long. In the previous chapters, techniques were given as to how to tackle it. This chapter will suggest a formal attempt to quell this problem by proposing a ten-session discipleship program. It is not the unique way for solving the early exit issue, but it can be a good beginning for churches that truly want to deal with this dilemma.

Being intentional in doing evangelism in the congregation where this program has been implemented, a new approach was adopted in the life of the church. This technique first put great emphasis on a pre-assimilation process where the church makes itself known in the community through felt-needs programs. Secondly, after new believers have joined the church, it embraced an assimilation phase to facilitate their involvement and their commitment to Christ. The third step, post-assimilation, set the goal to create what experts call production evangelism—the believer becomes disciple makers. As stated by Kidder in his book, *The Big Four*, we need to equip and motivate the laity to do great things for God. A growing church is not a one-person show.[1] Production evangelism (discipleship) helps to fight spiritual obesity in the church.

On December 7, 2013, a special party was organized to conclude the simple Bible study class for the newly baptized. A registration form was passed that day for a ten-week seminar on discipleship. Of the 39 new believers present at the event, 32 registered to attend the program. After remittance of the consent form one week prior to the launching (see Appendix A), the number dropped to 23 and then passed at 18 on the start day. The focus group was composed of 15 adults (nine women and six men), and three adolescents (two males, one female). In addition, another group comprised of nine ministry leaders (Sabbath school, visitation team, prayer ministry, fellowship group, hospitality, literature distribution, Bible study, youth and recreation group, teaching, and music) attended the entire seminar. From the 27 participants, only the 18 new converts were part of the project under study.

Before officially starting this project, a support group for new converts was created, a special training class on how to deal with new converts was conducted for the old members. Several sermons on love, the importance for Christians to bear fruit, and human relationships were preached consecutively to the entire body. The objectives were to make new converts proud of being a Christian, know more about Christ, and become disciples. Let us take a moment to underline the purpose of the support group. When someone accepts Jesus-Christ, gets baptized, and becomes a member of the church, it is not the end of their journey. On the contrary, it is just the beginning. It is a major transition in the life of that person. Because transitions are generally difficult, some might get discouraged, burnt out, feel misunderstood, and even abandon the faith. The support group for the newly baptized was created to provide all needed support to newly baptized members of the church in order to make the transition to their new life much easier. Their mission is to help the new believers integrate in the church community in a smooth, caring, easy way in order to help them move from the stage of simply member to that of disciple. The vision is to see that all new converts stay in church, get involved through mission and service, and develop a strong and intimate relationship with Jesus-Christ.

Collection of Data

The qualitative research method was used in this project for data collection. It is qualitative in the sense that it involves the examination and interpretation of observations for the purpose of finding meanings and patterns of relationships. Data were collected at the church where the program has taken place in the following ways: personal observation, questionnaires, pastoral visits, and surveys.

Each active participant in the project was administered a pre-test at the beginning and a post-test at the end. The overall questions covered three specific areas in five categories. The first area was generalities on discipleship to assess the understanding of new converts on discipleship. The second area was personal process of discipleship, and the third put accent on community process of discipleship. Area two, consisted of three different sets of questions (loving, understanding, and ministering), and area three of one set (equipping). (See Appendix B for list of questions)

The Project and Implementation

The project consisted of ten two-hour sessions and was conducted at the designated Church:

- Pre-test and General introduction on Discipleship
- Theoretical Foundation of Discipleship
- Christ and Discipleship
- The Holy Spirit and Discipleship
- God's Word and Discipleship
- Salvation and Discipleship
- Prayer and Discipleship
- Church and Discipleship
- Stewardship and Discipleship
- Project Review and Post-test

These modules were presented on the ladder of three basic characteristics of discipleship, which are teaching, mentoring (coaching), and witnessing on the following dates:

Session I: April 12, 2014 (3:00-5:00 P.M.)

Pre-test and Introduction

The registration process being completed, each participant having received their name tag, the project officially started on April 12, 2014 at three o'clock in the afternoon. It was an awesome moment anticipated for about five months. The participants were very excited, and the fellowship hall of the church contained thirty people; the presenter, the senior pastor, and the first elder of the church; eighteen new converts (active participants), and nine ministry leaders (adherent participants). After devotion, an informal but friendly presentation was made, and the pre-test (see Appendix B) was administered to the active participants.

Prior to the general introduction on discipleship, a total of nine small groups were created for panel discussion. Each small group comprised of a ministry leader serving as mentor and of two new converts (mentees). Great emphasis has been put on the importance of discipleship on that day. After the lecture, the small group panel discussion was convened where mentors and mentees reflected together on the theme by a series of questions and answers. Then, they prayed together in their specific groups. The presenter then answered some pertinent questions on discipleship. For example, he defined discipleship as a radical call to a total surrender to Christ. It is self denial and making Christ the top priority of one's life. He also states that discipleship requires intentionality and involves persistence, training, and sacrifice. The discipleship principle was summed up in the following words: "Jesus Above All." The participants expressed their satisfaction and reiterated their commitments. The first gathering was concluded as indicated in the daily format with the closing prayer of the senior pastor.

Session II: April 19, 2014 (3:00 – 5:00 P.M.)

Theoretical Foundations of Discipleship

The second lecture was focused on biblical, historical, and theological foundations of discipleship. These three main pillars upon which discipleship is based are described in chapters one, two, and three respectively. The presentation of each foundation was followed by a series of questions and answers in the small group panel discussion. This lecture was extremely important because it really set the tone for the seminar. After the lecture, the participants came to the understanding that discipleship is not optional but rather mandatory. The small groups were very animated; questions such as, how long it takes to be a disciple, how to become a productive disciple, etc, were at the center of the participants' debate? Because of their new comprehension of the subject, the seminarians committed not to miss any of the remaining presentations.

Session III: April 26, 2014 (3:00 – 5:00 P.M.)
Christ and Discipleship
The third gathering began with the devotional part and a brief review of the previous subject. This lecture helped the new convert understand that they have committed to Christ, who is their perfect model. They needed to remain faithful as they accomplish the work of a true disciple until Christ's return. They do not become mature as soon as they accept Christ as their personal Savior. "The journey of a disciple is a lifetime experience."[2] The participants also discovered that Christ's invitations, follow me (Mt 8:22) and abide in me (Jn 15:4), were not temporary but rather permanent. They also understood that each person functions and grows best in union with Christ. If they wish to bear fruit as required in the Word of God, they must remain connected to Christ, the Fruit-Bearer. "Abide in me as I abide in you. Just as the branch cannot bear fruit by itself unless it abides in the vine, neither can you unless you abide in me. I am the vine, you are the branches. Those who abide in me and I in them bear much fruit, because apart from me you can do nothing (Jn 15: 4, 5)." This lecture unequivocally cleared the participants' minds that Jesus is the Lord of discipleship; He called them to be not church members but His disciples with the responsibility to bring the unsaved to the Lordship of their Master. During this presentation, emphasis has been also put on obedience, which is one of the qualities of a true disciple. Christ was always obedient to His Father; new converts were taught to emulate Jesus in all details. He lived to glorify His heavenly Father. They were reminded that one of the best ways to praise God and to be a productive disciple is to bear good fruit as stated by Jesus Himself: "By this My Father is glorified, that you bear much fruit; so you will be My disciples (Jn 15: 8)."

Session IV: May 3, 2014 ((3:00 – 5:00 P.M.)

The Holy Spirit and Discipleship

The fourth meeting took place in a much-debated environment. Participants began to ask questions about the previous topic even before the devotional moment. In this segment, the new convert learned that they are not alone in their spiritual journey. Christ promised a comforter that is the Holy Spirit. He will guide and teach them all they need to know for their salvation. "In concluding the great commission with these words, I am with you always, Christ is providing his unlimited authority and his presence to assure the success of our mission of making disciples."[3] This presentation brought encouragement to new converts in their walk with Jesus when they discovered that the Savior had already made provision for them through the ministry of the Holy Spirit. Not only have the attendees understood the necessity of having this power, but they were also exhorted that He is available to all of them and that they just need to claim Him. In fact, Jesus Himself needed and received the Holy Spirit at His baptism. Therefore, it is imperative that we also receive the Holy Spirit, because a believer without the power of the Holy Spirit in their life is as weak as a new born babe. This lecture concluded with the clear comprehension that we cannot understand the Bible and all the truth without the presence of the Holy Spirit. The ah-ha moment for the participants was when they were told that God makes the Holy Spirit available and that they can claim Him right away. There cannot be discipleship without the presence and the empowerment of the Holy Spirit. God's Spirit is available to all those who are called to discipleship. Several questions were asked and the commitment for daily seeking the power of the Holy Spirit was made by all the attendees in their respective small group panel discussion.

Session V: May 10, 2014 (3:00 – 5:00 P.M.)

God's Word and Discipleship

The fifth presentation started with an inspiring devotion led by the senior pastor. After a quick review of the previous topic, much attention was directed toward God's love letter, which is the Bible. This lecture taught the new convert to understand their need for studying the Bible. Without a clear comprehension of God's word, it will be very difficult to be effective representatives of Christ. This critical point is supported by Greg Ogden in his manual.

"Along with Jesus Christ as both our foundation and the builder on it, the written Word of God is fundamentally connected to establishing and laying foundations in a believer's life."[4] The new convert also learned how to begin studying the Bible. The practical part of this study was enhanced in the small group panel discussion where some key verses (Jn 5:39; Ps 119: 11, 105) constituted the point of interest. The participants were reminded that only the study of the Word of God can help them know Christ and lead them into a forever relationship with him. "You search the scriptures because you think that in them you have eternal life; and it is they that testify on my behalf (Jn 5: 39)." Not only have new converts realized the importance of the Scriptures but they have also understood it as God's manual to help them grow in their spiritual journey. The apostle Paul clearly supports this assertion as he advised the young Timothy, "and that from childhood you have known the Holy Scriptures, which are able to make you wise for salvation through faith which is in Christ Jesus. All Scripture is given by inspiration of God, and is profitable for doctrine, for reproof, for correction, for instruction in righteousness, that the man of God may be complete, thoroughly equipped for every good work (2 Ti 3: 15-17)." To be authentic growing disciples, new converts must abide in the Word of God according to Jesus. "Then Jesus said to those Jews who believed Him, ""If you abide in my word, you are my disciples indeed"" (Jn 8: 31)."

Session VI: May 24, 2014 (3:00 – 5:00 P.M.)
Salvation and Discipleship
On the sixth day, emphasis was put on a fundamental doctrinal theme, which is salvation. This lecture was designed to help the new convert overcome the guilty feelings of sin and know that their salvation is guaranteed in Christ. Jesus has already paid the price of their redemption through his sacrificial death. The participants discovered that salvation is not something that money can buy. It is a gift from God, but we need to accept it. In addition, several attendees testified that was the first time they knew that Jesus means Savior. "In sharing human suffering, Jesus has become the pioneer and source of salvation to all who follow him (Heb 2:10; 5:9)."[5] As long as the new convert remains connected to Christ, their salvation is assured. They were also exhorted to avoid all extreme teachings about salvation: cheap grace, and salvation by

works. Christ, the root of salvation, will help them to produce good deeds, which are the fruit of salvation. "For by grace you have been saved through faith, and this is not your own doing; it is the gift of God—not the result of works, so that no one may boast. For we are what he has made us, created in Christ Jesus for good works, which God prepared beforehand to be our way of life (Eph 2: 8-10)."

Session VII: May 31, 2014 (3:00 – 5:00 P.M.)
Prayer and Discipleship
During the seventh gathering, more time was devoted to prayer. There is no spiritual life without prayer. "Prayer is our connection with God, our strength, and our bridge to heaven."[6] In this presentation, the new convert was taught the importance of prayer, which is the means of communication with God. They discovered they are not called to serve a distant God, but rather a God who hears and answers prayers. The participants were convinced they needed to imitate Christ in every aspect of His life. Like the twelve, not only do they need to ask Jesus to teach them to pray (Lk 11:1), but also they are exhorted to lead a life of prayer like their Master (Mk 1:35). Three times, the presentation was interrupted by special and specific moments of prayer. It was a remarkable day. Additional information about this presentation will be found in the Format/Handout distributed for this study in appendix C.

Session VIII: June 7, 2014 (3:00 – 5:00 P.M.)
Church and Discipleship
The eighth topic studied in this seminar was Church and Discipleship. After devotion and a brief review of the previous subject, emphasis was put on this particular theme. Some people say all they really need is Christ, but not the church. This lecture reminded the new convert of the importance of being part of Christ's body. Church is the place chosen by God for their spiritual growth and maturation and their preparation for heavenly dwelling. Jesus has placed them in the church to perfect their character for salvation. In his second volume, Luke clearly shows that Christ brings and keeps new converts in his church (Mt 16: 18). "Then those who gladly received his word were baptized; and that day about three thousand souls were added to them…And the Lord added to the church daily those who were being saved (Ac 2: 41, 47)."

Christ values His church. On his Damascus Road conversion experience, Jesus could have told Saul, later Paul, all he should have to do to become a useful and truthful disciple, but He rather sent him to a church leader to pray with him, to baptize and tell him what the Lord wanted him to know and do. Luke reports: "So he, trembling and astonished, said, "'Lord, what do You want me to do? Then the Lord said to him, "'Arise and go into the city, and you will be told what you must do.' And Ananias went his way and entered the house; and laying his hands on him he said, 'Brother Saul, the Lord Jesus, who appeared to you on the road as you came, has sent me that you may receive your sight and be filled with the Holy Spirit (Ac 9: 6, 17).'"

They also learned that the church is not the walls but rather the gathering of those that have been called by the Lord. Scope and nature of the church were also considered. Seen as a body and a bride, the church was compared to the ark of Noah. Only those who remained inside the ark were saved during the flood (see 1 Pt 3: 20; 2 Pt 2: 5). As such, participants were exhorted not to forsake their assemblies. The author of Hebrews makes this statement as clear as possible for all congregants as he writes, "Let us not give up meeting together, as some are in the habit of doing, but let us encourage one another, and all the more as you see the Day approaching (Heb 10: 25)." Going to and staying in church is fundamental to the growth process of a disciple. This is the place where you experience corporate worship, where your faith is strengthened by the proclamation of the Word of God, where you will find support and encouragement, and also where you can express your love for God and fellow human beings. No matter what, the Church is God's family on earth; as a disciple, you belong to it and must remain in it until Jesus comes to take you to heaven (see Jn 14: 1-3).

Session IX: June 14, 2014 ((3:00 – 5:00 P.M.)
Stewardship and Discipleship
The ninth gathering was particularly distinctive. After a quick revision of the prior topic, the presenter asked some random questions about stewardship. The participants were mostly ignorant about the topic. In this presentation, the new convert learned that God is the owner of all. As such, they are only stewards and must be faithful ones. They are to consecrate their time, talents, money (tithes and offerings), and their bodies to the Lord Jesus Christ. One

of the best ways for a disciple to be fruitful is to be healthy. Therefore, they are required to properly treat their bodies which are the temple of the Holy Spirit. "Do you not know that your body is a temple of the Holy Spirit, who is in you, whom you have received from God? You are not your own; you were brought at a price. Therefore honor God with your body (1 Cor. 6: 19, 20)." New converts were exhorted to avoid the consumption of prohibited foods, to eat moderately, and not to drink alcoholic beverages. The principles of a healthy living have been presented to them. Several questions asked about tithes and offerings, talents, and health principles were answered by the presenter before the closing of that session.

Session X: June 21 2014 (3:00 – 5:00 P.M.)
Project Review and Post-test
The entire seminar completed with a general overview of the program. Many unanswered questions were clarified on that day. This review was fundamental to the success of the project. The participants expressed their satisfaction by requesting other séances of training in order to learn more about discipleship. The presenter thanked all the attendees for their faithful and continuous presence and encouraged them to remain connected to Jesus, the Teacher par Excellence. The seminar concluded with the administration of the post-test. However, a 700-word essay was to be collected a week later. The last day of the seminar was quite different from the other days. A surprise dinner was organized on behalf of the participants by the support group for new converts. A basket of fruit to remind them as Christ's disciples the necessity to bear fruit, and a certificate of recognition and a brief summary of the twenty-eight fundamental beliefs of the Seventh-Day Adventists were given to each active participant. It was an amazing and unforgettable moment!

Analysis of Data
Qualitative data consist of words and observations, not numbers. As with all data, analysis and interpretation are required to bring order and understanding. The data in the study have been drawn from the active participants, new converts. Each active participant was given a pre-test survey at the initiation of the project. A 700-word essay was collected from them the week following the seminar. However, eight of them who were unable to write were given face-

to-face interviews. Finally, a post-test survey administered to the active participants concluded the project on June 21, 2014.

The pre- and post-test surveys had two parts. The first four questions were used to test how knowledgeable new converts were about discipleship, and also to evaluate any progress after attending the discipleship seminar. The twelve other questions were related to the four basic elements of discipleship, which are love, understanding the Word of God, ministering, and equipping. Those questions were actually the analysis tools of this project and were granted great consideration.

As shown in tables one to four, data from the post-test revealed a considerable level of comprehension of discipleship in comparison to the results found in the pre-test. For instance, question one defines discipleship as a passionate desire to follow Christ and to lead others to him as well; only one participant strongly agreed with that definition in the pre-test, meanwhile data in the post-test revealed ten participants strongly agreed with the very same definition. The findings showed that discipleship was viewed as a part of Christian life after the seminar. Post-test data, in question four, revealed sign of progress to become a disciple in comparison with the pre-test. For further detailed results regarding the sixteen questions, See Tables 1-16 in Appendix E.

Questions 5-7 were designed to discover how new converts had understood the concept of love after their baptism and also how important it is for a disciple to love God and his fellow human beings. In other words, love is the essence of discipleship. A new convert needs to relate intimately with God and develop positive relationships with others (Mt 22:36-37; Jn 13:35). Data from the tables in Appendix E have shown that new converts had a clearer understanding of the concept after attending the discipleship program. Questions 5 and 7 were to demonstrate their love to God and question six to their fellow human beings. Data from the post-test in question five (89%) compared to those in the pre-test (56%) indicated that the participants had a greater desire to love God. However, love for others was not so significant. It is true that an exhaustive report was not done for each individual; nonetheless, it is fair to admit that participants 3, 11, and 13 showed a very limited view of the concept even after the session.

Questions 8, 9, and 10 focused on the importance of the word of God. The new convert as a disciple is supposed to learn the truth of God's relationship with humanity through Jesus Christ, the Word of God (Jn 1:1; Mt 4:4). As stated by Jesus himself, the best way to know him is through the study of the Scriptures (Jn 5:39). Data shown in the post-test in comparison to the pre-test were very encouraging. They revealed in the pre-test that the Bible was not quite understood, and showed a more convincing comprehension of the Word of God in the post-test. For example, in the pre-test (question eight), 44% of the participants thought God does not love them because of their sins; however, data in the post-test revealed that 83% believed that God still loves them even though they sin. This section presented another reality about church and fellowship that is expressed in question 9. In the pre-test, only six participants strongly agreed that the church is God's family on earth. Data in the post-test revealed eleven, which is a considerable number.

Questions 11, 12, and 13 aimed at discovering the aptitude of new converts toward ministering to others or doing mission activities. The new convert has the responsibility to participate in God's mission of revelation, reconciliation, and restoration (Mt 28:19; 25:40; 2 Cor5: 19). The pre-test data revealed that the participants were reluctant in ministering to others prior to the seminar; only five of them agreed they needed to engage in mission. Data from the post-test results showed a greater aptitude toward missionary works; for thirteen of them strongly agreed that ministering to others is a vital component of a discipleship lifestyle. Responses from questions 11 and 13 in the post-test showed the participants' commitment to let others know about God (theology), while data from question 12 displayed their willingness to do mission (social work).

Finally, questions 14, 15, and 16 were designed to show the importance of equipping and how the participants would engage in learning activities to become more effective disciples of Christ. The new convert is perceived as a babe in faith, and as such they need to intentionally walk alongside other disciples for encouragement and equipping toward maturity in Christ (1 Pt2: 2; Eph 4: 15-16; Dt6: 4-9). Data in question 14 from the pre-test revealed that 83% of the participants were strongly interested in pastoral training. In the post-test, 89% of them showed their interests for on-going formation. There was no great change in their willingness to training. Data from Tables 15 and 16 reveals their strong desire to be around those who can help them grow in their spiritual journey. Data from the pre-test to post-test indicates that family worship and having religious friends went up from 67% to 94%, and from 72% to 89% respectively.

The lectures and questions were conceived in such a way to instill in each participant four basic and critical elements of discipleship (loving, understanding, ministering, and equipping). Each lecture encompassed these four fundamental elements of discipleship.

Discipleship is about deepening relationships. This view is well expressed by Thayer in her book, *Teaching for Discipleship*. The first element, which is love, "shows experiences that encourage people to grow in their relationship with Jesus Christ through personal and corporate Christian practices; to grow in self understanding; to grow in relationship with others."[7] In fact, Jesus presents love as the core element of discipleship. The apostle John helps us grasp this idea of the Master when he writes, "A new commandment I give to you, that you love one another; as I have loved you, that you also love one another. By this all will know that you are My disciples, if you have love for one another (Jn 13: 34, 35)."

Discipleship is not static but dynamic. The second element, understanding, was considered to help the participants to grow in a deeper knowledge of Jesus. It presented "experiences that give people new knowledge and understanding about Jesus and his teachings so that their love and obedience will increase."[8] The more we study the Scriptures, the better we know and understand Christ. "You search the Scriptures, for in them you think you have eternal life; and these are they which testify of Me (Jn 5: 39)." To grow and bear fruit as recommended by Jesus, the disciple must connect to Christ (Jn 15: 2, 4) and follow the growth steps prescribed by Peter in his second epistle (2 Pt 1: 5-11).

The third element, ministering, was selected to teach new converts that, upon acceptance of Christ as their Savior, they needed to engage in God's vineyard. It emphasized "experiences that provide opportunities for people to participate in God's mission by living out their call in service to others and in bearing their personal testimony about Christ."[9] Sharing the blessings of the Savior with others is part of the salvation package that Christ offers. This reality is well expressed in the life of the Gerasene demon-possessed man who requested to follow Jesus: "However, Jesus did not permit him, but said to him, 'Go home to your friends, and tell them what great things the Lord has done for you, and how He has had compassion on you.' And he departed and began to proclaim in Decapolis all that Jesus had done for him; and all marveled (Mk 5: 19, 20)."

The fourth element, equipping, was chosen on the basis of the apostle Paul's advice in Ephesians 4:12-13 to equip the saints for a more effective ministry. It displayed "experiences that encourage people to know, claim, and develop their gifts, discern God's call to them, and acquire the knowledge and skills needed to live out that call faithfully and effectively."[10] In regard to equipping the saints, Don James expresses similar concern: "When it comes to discipleship, everyone is a minister. Everyone needs to be equipped."[11]

The question analysis was done per category instead of on an each-question basis. Considering information from the tables, it sounds statistically logical to say that the overall data analysis from pre-test to post-test revealed significant improvement among the participants. Participant 17, for example, scored poorly in the pre-test when she had to define discipleship. She fully embraced the concept in the post-test. She admitted having misunderstood the term because there was in her hometown a religious group that called themselves disciples who seemed to use magical tactics to do physical healings. Participants 5 and 13 gave testimonials of how they slept well after the presentation on salvation. Participant 13 exclaimed "This is the very first time I am convinced I cannot earn my salvation. but Jesus offers it to me freely."

Outcome

The purpose of this project was to develop a Christ-based discipleship program that can help every new convert build a good, constant, personal, and spiritual relationship with Jesus. This goal could be reached through various specific objectives. The main objective of this ministry program was to help new converts become active participants in the church's life after their baptisms so they can be transformed from members to disciples.

The primary measurement of the outcome came from the data collected from the pre-test administered to the participants at the launching of the project. The measurement tool was their participation in different church activities. This information has been collected from the report provided by the adherent participants who mentored them and supervised their involvement in several church ministries. Personal observation, data from post-test and face-to-face interviews conducted have enhanced the outcome of this project. In the beginning, the involvement of new converts appeared very timid. However, throughout the program, significant progress has been noticed in the attitudes of new converts towards involvement in church activities. This tendency also has been revealed in the answers found in the participants' weekly evaluation forms.

In addition, it makes sense to report some other encouraging signs of involvement among the participants. During and after the program, church attendance increased due to invitations that new converts extended to their family members and friends. In fact, many of them have not only attended the church and participated in Bible study, but they have also given their hearts to Jesus through baptism. According to their own testimonies, several new converts testified that they did not leave the church early because of the support that they gained from their peers. Truly, the hypothesized outcome for this project, which was new converts' participation in church's life, has been attained at a considerable level.

Triangulation

To check and establish validity in this project, data triangulation was utilized. Three sets of data were considered, survey (questionnaire), 700-word essay, and face-to-face interviews. Five categories (patterns) and coding were used in the triangulation process: love for God and fellow human beings (L), understanding of the Word of God (U), ministering (M), equipping (E), and networking (N). Results obtained from these sources of collection revealed the emergence of these patterns in the data. There were consistencies among the selected categories in each set of data collected. The triangulation showed agreed outcomes. For instance, the category love (L) appeared at 89%, 80%, and 88% respectively in the questionnaire, 700-word essay, and face-to-face interviews. Thus, it is likely that these outcomes are true. Like the other categories, love has been a critical factor in the discipleship accepting among the participants (new converts). More statistical information about these patterns can be found in Table 17 in Appendix E.

Credibility

Information collected in the 700-word essay, and face-to-face interviews from the participants have shown great interest from them in the study. As such, the results were judged credible because the participants are the best-qualified people to judge the credibility of this project.

Transferability

Pastors of several other congregations in the United States have been contacted and encouraged to implement this project in their churches. They have all found and concluded that it is workable. Therefore, there has been no doubt in regard to the transferability of this discipleship program in other denominational churches.

Dependability

This project utilized a qualitative methodology approach. There is no need for estimating its reliability in measuring it twice. However, the results obtained prove a change in the attitudes and behaviors of the participants in regard to their involvement in church activities and their understanding of discipleship through the following basic elements: love, understanding, ministering, and equipping.

Confirmability

Confirmability refers to the degree to which the results could be confirmed or corroborated by others. This procedure has been documented throughout the study as data have been checked and rechecked for at least three times. Data from the triangulation table are a proven source of confirmability.

The task of this current chapter was to describe the program's application, and to present the results, implications, and influence upon ministry at the selected church. In the next chapter, in-depth reflection and consideration will be given to exhibit a more exhaustive comprehension of the project and its implementation

---

1: S. Joseph Kidder, *The Big Four: Secrets to a Thriving Church Family* (Hagerstown, MD: Review and Herald Publishing Association, 2011), 54.

2: Jane Thayer, *Teaching for Discipleship: Strategies for Transformational Learning* (Unpublished, 2009), 4.

3: Jane Thayer, *Teaching for Discipleship: Strategies for Transformational*

Learning (Unpublished, 2009), 10.

4: Greg Ogden, *Unfinished Business: Returning The Ministry to the People of God* (Grand Rapids, MI: Zondervan, 2003), 147.

5: Ivan T. Blazen, *Handbook of Seventh-day Adventist Theology*, vol. 12. Edited by George W. Reid, Commentary Reference (Hagerstown, MD: Review and Herald Publishing Association, 2000), 271.

6: Ellen G. White, *Power of Prayer,* (New York, NY: TEACH Services, Inc., 1994), iii.

7: Jane Thayer, *Teaching for Discipleship: Strategies for Transformational Learning* (Unpublished, 2009), 18.

8: Jane Thayer, *Teaching for Discipleship: Strategies for Transformational Learning* (Unpublished, 2009), 18.

9: Jane Thayer, *Teaching for Discipleship: Strategies for Transformational Learning* (Unpublished, 2009), 18.

10: Jane Thayer, *Teaching for Discipleship: Strategies for Transformational Learning* (Unpublished, 2009), 18.

11: Don James, *Orientation to Holistic Groups and the Journey of Discipleship* (Berrien Springs, MI: Open Home Ministries, 2005), 41.

CHAPTER ELEVEN
REFLECTIONS, SUGGESTIONS,
AND CONSIDERATIONS

Christ's goal has always been to make disciples. "When Jesus was on earth, He interacted with many people in different ways, from one-on-one teaching to preaching to multitudes. He called to Himself a select group of twelve men known as His disciples. All Jesus did to teach these men His way was to draw them close to Himself. That simplicity should still be used today."[1] As God's ambassador on earth, the church needs to be intentional in ways and methods to bring people to Jesus and to keep them. In other terms, in order for the church to lead people into a deeper relationship with Christ, they need to know that they are loved, their felt-needs will be met, and that their talents will be used.

As per Jesus' method, the best way to make new converts become disciples is to draw them close to ourselves. We cannot help the new believers have a good relation with Christ without mingling with them and teaching them the ways to do that. This program has been designed to create this atmosphere of closeness with new converts, to enhance their involvement in the church's life, and to help them build a strong and constant relationship with Jesus. The church has the moral obligation to connect new converts to Christ so they can become His disciples. This connection is made possible through prayer and study of the Word. Teaching and encouraging the new believers to daily spend quality time with the Savior and search the Scriptures will lead them in the path to becoming mature disciples. That will also help them discover not a master-slave relationship with Jesus, but rather a Savior-friend relationship. In the process of making disciples, it is critical that the postulants realize that they are about to enter into a friendly and loving relationship with Christ.

The conception of this project was a hazardous attempt because it was the first time such an initiative was undertaken in this particular congregation. The implementation presented great challenges; the fear of failures was constant throughout all the phases. However, despite the initial fears and struggles, this project has been one of the most rewarding experiences for this ecclesial community and for the author as well.

The program at first aimed at the participation of new converts in church activities to facilitate their retention. The implementation phase of the project started with eighteen active participants (new converts) and concluded with the same number. Achieving a one hundred participation rate among new converts registered was greatly encouraging. Participants were required to complete a participant's evaluation at the end of each topic. These evaluations are one of the main tools used to evaluate the effectiveness of this project. Based upon the answers given by both active participants (new converts) and adherent participants (ministry leaders) on the evaluations, it is evident that this Christ-based discipleship program was successful at aiding in the development of new converts' spiritual maturity toward a strong relationship with Christ as they discovered their place of ministry within the church.

The project was designed to give active participants a deeper appreciation for their faith, a positive image of themselves for being Christ's followers, a love for the church, and a clear comprehension of the call of Jesus. It was also meant to enable new converts to see themselves as productive disciples in God's field instead of simple religious consumers. The hope was that this new perceptive would change their attitudes and behaviors. In fact, throughout the seminar the participants were taught that ministry is not the work of the pastor only. New converts, upon accepting Christ as their personal Savior, should engage in the work of salvation through witnessing, mission, and service. The apostle Peter made witnessing an integral part of new converts' duty in his first letter. "But you are a chosen people, a royal priesthood, a holy nation, God's special possession, that you may declare the praises of him who called you out of darkness into his wonderful light (1 Pt 2: 9)." Marlene Wilson, writing about a theology of the priesthood of all the believers, states this view even more clearly in her book, *How to Mobilize Church Volunteers*: "Ministry is the work of the whole priesthood, and it involves being called by the Holy Spirit to do six things: proclaim, teach, worship, love, witness, and serve."[2] On his part, Kidder, quoting Ellen G. White, expresses "that it is the duty of the ministers to teach the members how to labor in the church and in the community."[3]

In regard to involvement, notices of participation were made. According to reports from ministry leaders and personal observation, several participants were willing to pray aloud during Wednesday night meetings. It was also reported that some answered questions without hesitation at their Sabbath school class, and others when they were asked participated in the reading of biblical passages and other ministries. The primary objective of the project dealt with transforming new converts from members to disciples. Hearing testimonies of church officers made the project meaningful. The success of this project has been the result of a combined effort. The approval of the church board, the willingness of the church ministry leaders, and the unconditional participation of new converts were remarkable. At the same time, it is wise to admit that being a disciple is a lifelong journey of transformation. Teaching for a change in attitudes and behaviors is a complicated process that requires a long-term mind-set. Though more work needs to be done, there is clear evidence that making disciples is not an impossible task.

Biblical/Theological Reflections

Discipleship requires not perfection but willingness to learn and spend quality time with the Master. "Even though Jesus was the teacher sent from God, it took Him time to make disciples of those who followed Him. He was working with people who were less than perfect. Jesus and the disciples walked together and the lessons grew out of real life situations."[4] The relational aspect experienced by the participants in the small group discussion panel was in harmony with the biblical principles found in the book of Acts. They continually devoted themselves to the apostles' teaching and to fellowship, to the breaking of bread and to prayer (Acts 2:42). This verse depicts the fellowship of the believers in the early church.

A key element of success in this project was punctuality. Participants knew there was a time to start and a fixed period to end. This was made possible through the fellowship system set in place during the seminar. After worship service ended, all the participants ate together and shared other issues. This helped them to better know one another and develop a real sense of brotherhood within the community. Time selection for the gatherings also played a critical role in the success of this project. The Sabbath belongs to God (Exodus 20:9). It was therefore much easier to find and gather all the participants in the church on the day and time previously selected.

This project helped to grasp a better understanding of the Great Commission that Jesus gave to His disciples before His ascension. It reminds us that being a disciple is not optional but mandatory and has eternal consequences. In the case of Jesus' final assignment, we often think that if new converts have accepted Jesus as their Savior and understand the basic doctrines of the church, this knowledge will lead them into a close walk with Christ. This way of thinking is false and needs to be corrected. "The job of the church consists of making disciples. It will take time, but it is normal; for the Gospels portray Christ's disciples as slow learners."[5]

Making disciples is the central assignment included in the Great Commission, and the church does not need to wait months and years to start doing it. "Every true disciple is born into the kingdom of God as a missionary. The receiver becomes a giver."[6] Thayer explains this idea very well in her book titled, *Teaching for Discipleship*: "The so-called Great Command links a relationship with God and a relationship with other human beings. Love God with all your heart and soul and mind and your neighbor as yourself (Matt.22: 37-38)."[7] The outcome of this loving relationship is bearing fruit. If we do not bear fruit, we fail to satisfy Christ's expectation of every genuine disciple. In other terms, there is no discipleship without fruit-bearing. The Savior has chosen us not only to develop a growing relationship with Him but also to go and bear fruit. Christ plainly clarifies this stance in the Gospel of John: "You did not choose Me, but I chose you and appointed you that you should go and bear fruit, and that your fruit should remain, that whatever you ask the Father in My name He may give you (Jn 15: 16)." It is worth elucidating that a disciple does not bear fruit to be saved; for there is only one means of salvation, which is Jesus and Jesus alone (Ac 4: 12). Bearing fruit is evidence that the disciple is connected to the fruit-bearer, which is Christ (Jn 15: 5).

Some individuals wonder and speculate about the fruit the disciples are supposed to bear in John 15. Others make allusion to the fruit(s) of the Spirit cited in Galatians 5. However, the context, in which this part of Christ's discourse was given, leaves no doubt that Jesus was talking about sharing the good news with others (See Mt 28: 19; Mk 16:15). Jesus was asking the eleven disciples to bear fruit. Like produces like. In other words, He was telling them to go and make disciples like them. Thus, John's immediate context is making disciples of all nations; bearing fruit equates making disciples. The fruit(s) of the Spirit in Galatians 5 enable us to become more competent, efficient, and effective in our mission and task of discipleship. The kind of fruit the disciples are called to bear in Jn 15, particularly verse 16, is producing disciples. And the key to bear fruit or making disciples is to remain connected to Christ, dwell in Him, and allow Him and His Word dwell in us (Jn 15: 4-6). There is no child without intimate contact. Likewise, there is no fruit-bearing without an intimate, obedient, and loving relationship with Christ (Jn 15: 5).

Eschatological Reflection

Christ did not give the church the responsibility to make church members but rather disciples. All baptized people are chosen to be disciples of Christ. The church has the duty to train and help them grow to become mature. The best way to reach this maturity and spiritual growth is through the sharing of Christ with others. The Great Commission is linked to witnessing to non-believers as they become followers. The Second Coming of Christ and the end of the world go hand in hand with discipleship. One of the final and distinctive signs given that precede Jesus' second return is the preaching of the gospel. However, according to the Synoptic Gospels, who is responsible for preaching the good news? The disciples are. This is the fundamental reason for the church to make disciples. In other terms, as members are being transformed into disciples, more lost people will be able to know about Jesus, the Savior. As these disciples preach the gospel, the Holy Spirit will empower them, and the church will experience an exponential growth. The number of the elect will be complete, and Jesus' prophecies concerning His Second Coming will be fulfilled, in particular that found in the book of Matthew: "And this gospel of the kingdom will be preached in the whole world as a testimony to all nations, and then the end will come (Mt 24: 14)."

If we are tired of living in this sinful world, we must be interested in sharing the good news with the unsaved. In fact, among all the signs that herald the Second Coming of Jesus, only the preaching of the gospel is unequivocally linked to the end of the world (Mt 24: 14b). When church members become disciples with the passion to fulfill the Great Commission, the next voice that we will soon hear will be that of Jesus, saying: "And behold, I am coming quickly, and My reward is with Me, to give to everyone according to his work (Rev 22: 12)."

Important Suggestions

The small group panel discussion has been a tremendous tool in the success of this project. It allows the attendees to give their inputs, which are at times very significant. Throughout the implementation of the project, some adjustments were made. For instance, the weekly report was not part of the initial conception. However, after the first presentation, a participant came up with a question about the assignment for next meeting, and then the weekly report became a requirement. It has helped keep the participants on the track and made them appear more collaborative. The idea of a weekly report was suggested by one of the adolescent active participants, approved by the presenter, and backed by almost 90% of the overall attendance. This suggestion was in line with the hypothesis formulated for the project. If new converts attend this discipleship seminar, they will show strong commitment toward Christ, become more mature, and get involved in church activities. This has been noticed at the launching of the program. This proposition appeared very mature and constituted an important tool for evaluating the effectiveness of the project.

The completion of this project has enabled us to see where it can be improved. Though they are new in the faith, one can draw many good ideas from new converts that will help prepare a more comprehensive and in-depth discipleship program. Suggestions made by the participants have been taken into consideration and utilized, and they will be used for further study. The result and suggestions revealed that mentorship should be an integral part to this program. Better and greater results will be gained when ministry leaders are trained as professional mentors. To be successful, a Christ-centered discipleship program or model must create formal small groups for in-depth and interactive study. The curriculum has instituted a small group panel discussion comprised of three individuals: one ministry leader and two active participants (new converts). As they expressed the joy coming from these small groups, the participants suggested that there should be at least four-to-six people in each group. These groups created a feeling of fellowship and promoted a sense of community within the body. These small groups have been seen as key to building relationships with one another.

Considerations

Christ has given us the mission of making disciples. We need to understand that discipleship cannot stand alone. In his book, *Christ's Way of Making Disciples*, Samaan expresses this view with clarity. "Witnessing and disciple-making must always remain linked together. Adding new converts must be followed up with multiplying fruit-bearing disciples."[8] This project has convincingly shown there are several steps to take in order to develop a successful Christ-based discipleship program.

First of all, we must imitate Christ's method. It is the only strategy that gives true success. Samaan presented six steps taken by the Master to reach others. "Jesus' mingling with others as one who (1) desired their good, (2) sympathized with them, (3) ministered to their needs, (4) won their trust, (5) bade them to follow him, and (6) made them fishers of men."[9] These steps lead to the understanding that the church needs to be intentional in doing evangelism if they want to build a Christ-based discipleship model for new converts. We must be first disciples of Jesus before we can make disciples for Christ. One can teach what they know but cannot reproduce who they are not. Thus, it is impossible to make disciples if we ourselves are not disciples. If the church wants to fulfill the mandate of the Great Commission, they must have and maintain a culture of discipleship within it.

Developing a successful Christ-based discipleship program for new converts requires that the congregation do community outreach activities to meet people's needs. There is no effective discipleship model without practical and intentional witnessing. Those who benefit from these felt-needs programs offered by the church will easily join the new community of faith in accepting Jesus as their personal Savior. New converts then receive training and formation to become disciples and disciple-makers. This must be a continuous process or activity in the life of the church until Christ returns. In their book,

Finding Them, Keeping Them, McIntosh and Martin presented "five effective strategies to lead people to Christ (Be present in the community, Proclaim the gospel, Persuade people to accept Christ, Help people progress in their Christian life, and Help people produce new believers)."[10] The last two strategies go in harmony with this volume, helping new converts to become mature in their relationship with Christ through training and equipping so they can be disciple-makers for Christ. They also pinpoint the link between evangelism and discipleship. Jones, indeed, argues that "evangelism is to be understood as an aspect of the church's mission that seeks to help persons enter into Christian discipleship."[11]

The implementation of this project has revealed something very significant about training. It has permitted to identify the spiritual gifts of many participants. In this context, Kidder, citing Ellen G. White, wrote "the pastors should first train the members to do evangelism so that the whole church can minister together."[12] As a result of this training, he goes on to say that "all churches should make sure that people are in the proper place in their ministry, as God has made them and wired them."[13] It is difficult to realize such goals without conducting a spiritual gifts assessment in the church.

There is so much to learn to become a disciple. Discipleship is a lifelong activity. This project has been designed to introduce new converts to the discipleship world. There is no pretention that an exhaustive study was done. Several biblical doctrines were not covered due to the length of this project. It is evident that new converts who become disciples need to know much more so that they can be transformed into disciple-makers. Much research can be done to display a wider understanding of the concept; there is room for improvement. Not all the objectives were attained in the short-term, but most of them have been achieved. There are hopeful signs that new converts can be transformed from members to Disciples. Indeed, three years after the implementation of this program, we keep getting great news from the participants about their involvement inside and outside the church. Discipleship is truly reproduction or multiplication of who Christ wants you to be.

A summary thought about a successful discipleship program is to turn the postulants' eyes to Jesus, teaching them to obey and submit themselves to the Master. They must not focus on temporary reward but on the final one, which Christ will give at the consummation of all things at his return. Jesus requires self-denial from all of his disciples (Lk 14: 27) and teaches that God must occupy the first place in their lives (Mt 6: 33). He does not promote an easy life but a tested one (Jn 16: 33). The encouraging factor is to remember that He has already overcome the evil one and promised to be with His disciples in the midst of their tribulations. The prophet Isaiah puts it this way, "Fear not, for I am with you; Be not dismayed, for I am your God. I will strengthen you, Yes, I will help you, I will uphold you with my righteous right hand (Is 41: 10)." Spiritually speaking, making disciples is not an easy task, but the One who has called us is and will be with His followers. "Now the Lord spoke to Paul in the night by a vision, ""Do not be afraid, but speak, and do not keep silent; for I am with you, and no one will attack you to hurt you; for I have many people in this city""" (Ac 18: 9-10)." No matter what, a believer must be at work as soon as they enroll in Christ's discipleship school. Christ has set the example (Jn 9: 4), and Paul has applied it immediately following his baptism. "Immediately there fell from his eyes something like scales, and he received his sight at once; and he arose and was baptized. So when he had received food, he was strengthened. Then Saul spent some days with the disciples at Damascus. Immediately he preached the Christ in the synagogues, that He is the Son of God (Ac 9: 18-20).

1: Jane Thayer, Teaching for Discipleship: Strategies for Transformational Learning (Unpublished, 2009), 2.

2: Marlene Wilson, *How to Mobilize Church Volunteers* (Minneapolis, MN: Augsburg Publishing House, 1983), 15.

3: S. Joseph Kidder, *The Big Four: Secrets to a Thriving Church Family* (Hagerstown, MD: Review and Herald Publishing Association, 2011), 57.

4: Jane Thayer, Teaching for Discipleship: Strategies for Transformational Learning (Unpublished, 2009), 16.

5. Jane Thayer, Teaching for Discipleship: Strategies for Transformational Learning (Unpublished, 2009), 16.

6: Ellen G. White, *Christian Service* (Hagerstown, MD: Review and Herald Publishing Association, 2002), 9.

7: Jane Thayer, Teaching for Discipleship: Strategies for Transformational Learning (Unpublished, 2009), 16.

8: Philip G. Samaan, *Christ's Way of Making Disciples* (Hagerstown, MD: Review and Herald Publishing Association, 1999), 10.

9: Philip G. Samaan, *Christ's Way of Making Disciples* (Hagerstown, MD: Review and Herald Publishing Association, 1999), 10.

10: Gary McIntosh & Glen Martin, Finding Them, Keeping Them: Effective Strategies for Evangelism and Assimilation in the Local Church (Nashville, TN: Publishing Group, 1992), 13-15.

11: Scott J. Jones, The Evangelistic Love of God & Neighbor: A Theology of Witness & Discipleship (Nashville, TN: Abingdon Press, 2003), 65.

12: S. Joseph Kidder, *The Big Four: Secrets to a Thriving Church Family* (Hagerstown, MD: Review and Herald Publishing Association, 2011), 57.

13: S. Joseph Kidder, *The Big Four: Secrets to a Thriving Church Family* (Hagerstown, MD: Review and Herald Publishing Association, 2011), 57.

CHAPTER TWELVE

CONCLUSION

The idyllic result of this discipleship program would be to see all new converts becoming disciples. Unfortunately, this did not happen immediately for all; some participants have not entirely embraced the discipleship concept yet. The expected outcome of this project was that all new converts have a good knowledge of Christ and get involved in church ministry. Based on the results revealed by the data, great progress has been made, though the project has been a work in process. The program was a short-term endeavor designed to introduce new converts to the discipleship world. However, the preliminary results show not only the positive response of numerous neophytes but also the feasibility of a discipleship model for the church in general and the new believers in particular. It is encouraging to see several new converts willing to share Jesus with others. Listening to their intervention in the small group panel discussion allows the conclusion that the seminar was successful. They now view discipleship as their loving response to the incommensurable love of God for humankind.

"A comprehensive understanding of discipleship is incomplete until it incorporates a passionate desire to follow Jesus and, as a supernatural result, a passionate desire to lead others to Christ, as well."[1] Four areas of discipleship have been selected to measure the success of this project: involvement in regular worship services through presence and participation, commitment to God's word through regular reading and study of the Bible, financial contribution to God's work through tithes and offerings, and involvement in God's work through evangelism and mission. Some good and encouraging reports about the program have been submitted; however, the full accomplishment of these measurements requires time and patience.

Discipleship is a long-term approach. The project has provided some basic information for new converts, but discipleship is so much more than information. It is a lifestyle, a lifelong process of apprentice, growth, and change. All that could not happen in such a short period of time. Becoming a productive disciple takes time. Thayer is correct when she writes, "A relationship with Christ is not naturally the most basic human need; it becomes the most basic need through supernatural intervention, the grace of God."[2] Discipleship is the fulfillment of the two greatest commandments, love for God and for our fellow human beings (Mt 22: 37-39). Discipleship is all about love (agape), self-sacrifice love for God, and love for our neighbors. True love for God is manifested in obedience and the keeping of His commandments (Jn 15:10). Genuine love for our neighbors is revealed in the sharing of the good news of salvation with them.

Even though all the expected outcomes are not met yet in the short term, attempting to develop and implement a discipleship program aiming at transforming new converts from members to disciples of Christ is a worthwhile endeavor. This attempt is in line with Thayer's assertion in her unpublished work, *Teaching for Discipleship*, when she writes that "the making of disciples should be the central purpose of every Christian church."[3] She goes on to say that "a person does not become mature in Christ as soon as she accepts Christ as her Savior. The journey of a disciple is a lifetime experience as it is expressed by James. Discipleship does not stop at baptism, but continues on with mentoring, friendship evangelism, and leadership, until we meet Jesus face to face at that great second coming."[4]

It is our responsibility to teach them God's grace and make them disciples. To be productive disciples, new converts need to be equipped as well. Mentioning the roles and responsibility of the pastor, Greg Ogden writes: "With the elders, the pastor is to encourage the people in their worship and service; to equip and enable them for their tasks within the Church and their mission to the world...and its task in reaching out in concern and service to the life of the human community as a whole."[5] That was exactly one of the main goals of this project, equipping new converts so that they can be transformed from members to Disciples of Christ.

We are serving a missionary God. After the fall, He launched his first missionary trip to rescue Adam and Eve from eternal destruction. He later commissioned Noah to bring and share the good news of salvation with the Antediluvian society. They unfortunately rejected his offer of salvation. Then He called the patriarch Abraham to be a blessing for all nations in propagating the knowledge of the True and Unique God. After witnessing the sufferings and hearing the cries of the Israelites in Egypt, Moses was sent for their deliverance. Throughout the Old Testament, God kept sending missionaries through the ministry of his prophets. The Inter-Testament period was concluded with the sending of the missionary work of John the Baptist. The New Testament period began with the launching of the greatest divine missionary activity, which is the sending of the Son of God with the mission to seek and save the lost. That was indeed Christ's mission statement as reported by Luke: "For the Son of Man has come to seek and to save that which was lost (Lk 19: 10)." The beloved disciple John on his part corroborated the Lukan missionary view as he writes in his gospel, "For God did not send His Son into the world to condemn the world, but that the world through Him might be saved (Jn 3: 17)." The whole Bible is about a loving sending God.

Jesus was sent by His Father, and He obeyed. As disciples, we must follow Christ's steps. Before He sent us, Jesus confirmed that the Father had sent Him. So Jesus said to them again, "Peace to you! As the Father has sent Me, I also send you (Jn 20: 21)." Christ's sending mission to us is crystal clear: making disciples. "Go therefore and make disciples of all the nations, baptizing them in the name of the Father and of the Son and of the Holy Spirit, teaching them to observe all things that I have commanded you; and lo, I am with you always, even to the end of the age (Mt 28: 19, 20)." It is worth noting that Christ did not ask us to make simply converts or church members but disciples who should themselves bear fruit. "You did not choose Me, but I chose you and appointed you that you should go and bear fruit, and that your fruit should remain (Jn 15: 16)." Making disciples is not a one hundred percent human activity but a teamwork effort. Making disciples firstly requires the conversion of the unsaved, which is the work of the Holy Spirit. Therefore, the key to make disciples is a loving obedience, submission, and cooperation with the

Holy Spirit. When we do our part, the Holy Spirit will take care of the rest. Since Christ is the Master and the sender of the mission, then the mandate to make disciples is doable and possible.

We generally fail in making disciples because we forget to connect to the source. We fail because we try to make it on our own. We fail because we forget that we cannot do anything without Christ (Jn 15: 5). Christ will never ask us to do what is impossible. The secret in making disciples is to remember that Christ is the One who will make it in and through us. Yes, making disciples is possible because Jesus has promised to be with us (Mt 28: 20b), and He will certainly be because He has kept and will always keep His promises. Moses clearly states: "God is not a man, that He should lie, nor a son of man, that He should repent. Has He said, and will He not do? Or has He spoken, and will He not make it good (Nu 23: 19)?" Let us thus emulate Christ's way and method of making disciples, mingling with the lost, meeting their needs, baptizing and instructing them to follow all Christ's teachings. Let us claim the power of the Holy Spirit (Ac 1: 8), and then making disciples will be as easy as it was during the formation period of the early Christian church. It is good to be reminded that, whenever God asks a person to perform a work, He always makes His Spirit available to them. Read Exodus 31:1-11; 1Sa 16:11-13.

As for those who are called to enter the discipleship life, we must admit that being or becoming a disciple is very costly. It sometimes involves ridicule, mockery, and persecution of the world, and/or even the abandonment of the loved ones. It can cost you your job and position in society, and your physical life as well. In fact, it is reported that, except for the apostle John, all the other apostles of Christ were murdered. However, despite this alarming account, there is hope and good news for the true disciple. The apostle Paul, in his first letter to the Corinthians, gives a glimpse of what God has in store for the faithful disciples. But as it is written: "Eye has not seen, nor ear heard, nor have entered into the heart of man, the things which God has prepared for those who love Him (1 Co 2: 9)."

Yes, my friend, it is worth being a disciple of Christ; there is an amazing reward attached to it. If you are not fully convinced by Paul's assertion, put your trust in Jesus who cannot err and promises the greatest and incomparable interest rates to his disciples. To have a clearer idea, let us read how Jesus answers to Peter's apprehension in regard to those who become his followers.

"Then Peter said, ""See, we have left all and followed You.' So He said to them, ""Assuredly, I say to you, there is no one who has left house or parents or brothers or wife or children, for discipleship is the sake of the kingdom of God, who shall not receive many times more in this present time, and in the age to come eternal life"" (Lk 18: 28-30)."

Lastly, about sharing and blessed reciprocity: If you have been blessed by Jesus upon becoming His disciple, do not keep the blessing for yourself. Go and share the blessed hope of salvation with others like the Samaritan woman did. In so doing, you are a disciple and a disciple-maker. That is exactly what God expects from you. Like the patriarch Abraham, may all of us be a blessing for others. Then and then only will others discover the motivator God behind our kindness and our love. We will become fruit-bearing disciples and the love of God will be manifest in our lives. "By this we know that we love the children of God, when we love God and keep His commandments. For this is the love of God, that we keep His commandments. And His commandments are not burdensome (1 Jn 5: 2, 3)." There is no more time to waste; the end is near, and Jesus is coming soon. Let us go and tell it now to all nations in order to fulfill Jesus' mandate. Let us be obedient with the aim of seeking the lost, keeping them, and making them disciples!

1:   Dan Solis, *Discipleship: Adult Sabbath School Bible Study Guide*, (Nampa, ID: Pacific Press, Jan, Feb, Mar 2014), 3.

2:   Jane Thayer, *Teaching for Discipleship: Strategies for Transformational Learning* (Unpublished, 2009), 4.

3:   Jane Thayer, *Teaching for Discipleship: Strategies for Transformational Learning* (Unpublished, 2009), 9.

4:   Don James, *Orientation to Holistic Groups and the Journey of Discipleship* (Berrien Springs, MI: Open Home Ministries, 2005), 9.

5:   Greg Ogden, *Unfinished Business: Returning The Ministry to the People of God* (Grand Rapids, MI: Zondervan, 2003), 131.

CHAPTER THIRTEEN
BONUS: THE ULTIMATE COMEBACK
THE BLESSED HOPE OF CHRIST'S DISCIPLES

The events that we are living nowadays leave no doubt that our present world is nearing its end. The only blessed hope we have lies in the soon return of our Lord and Savior, Jesus Christ. One of the greatest evangelists that ever lived was Dwight L. Moody. Being so fascinated by this subject, it is reported that Moody decided to begin reading the Bible to see how often the Second Coming of Christ was mentioned. To his amazement, he found over 2,500 references! Therefore, it is useless to tell you that the Second Coming of Christ is one of the most important truths of the Bible. It is true that we are living in a dangerous world. It is true that we are facing daily natural catastrophes. It is true that the cost of living is getting higher and higher. It is true that immorality reaches its paroxysm. However, I am happy to say that things will not remain the same forever. Christ is coming again to put an end to this chaotic and alarming situation. Though the future of this world appears very dark, we are continually reminded of Christ's promises. "Behold, I am coming quickly, and My reward is with Me, to render to every man according to what he has done (Re 22: 12)."

Talking about the Second Coming of Christ signifies undoubtedly that He had come before. Indeed, He came as a babe in Bethlehem to die for our sins (Mi.5:1; Es.9:5, 6; 53:1-12). The religious people in Jesus' day had the

Old Testament of the Bible explaining exactly how Jesus would come, when He would come, and in what manner He would come. Everything happened as predicted. And yet the vast majority of religious people missed His first coming. Is the world different today? We can learn much from this, for history often repeats itself. The clear lesson from the past is, "Ready or not, Jesus is coming again." The first time, Jesus came to confirm God's promise to humankind (Gn 3: 15), to solve sin's problem (1 Jn 3: 8), to establish the kingdom of God (Mk 1: 15), to save the lost and the sinners (Lk 19: 10; 1 Ti 1: 15), and to set and leave an example of obedience (Jn 15: 10). The fulfillment of the ancient prophecies about His first coming should leave no doubt concerning His Second Coming.

Certainty of Christ's Second Coming
What does the Bible say about His return?

Many biblical characters, both New and Old Testaments, unequivocally mention Christ's Second Coming.

A1. Old Testament Faces:
Enoch prophesied, saying, "Behold, the Lord came with many thousands of His holy ones" (Jude 14).

The psalmist Asaph described His coming as follows: "May our God come and not keep silence; Fire devours before Him, And it is very tempestuous around Him (Ps 50: 3)."

The prophet Daniel tells the reason of his Second Coming: "And in the days of these kings the God of heaven will set up a kingdom which shall never be destroyed; and the kingdom shall not be left to other people; it shall break in pieces and consume all these kingdoms, and it shall stand forever (Da 2: 44)."

A2. New Testament Faces:
Paul prophesied that Jesus will come from heaven: "For the Lord Himself will descend from heaven with a shout, with the voice of an archangel, and with the trumpet of God. And the dead in Christ will rise first (1 Th 4: 16)."

Peter tells the manner of Christ's return: "But the day of the Lord will come as a thief in the night, in which the heavens will pass away with a great noise, and the elements will melt with fervent heat; both the earth and the works that are in it will be burned up (2Pt 3: 10)."

John shows no indefinite delay: "He who testifies to these things says, ""Surely I am coming quickly.' Amen. Even so, come, Lord Jesus (Re 22: 20)!"

A3. Heavenly Beings:
The Angels proclaim that Jesus will come back the same way He went to heaven. They say, "Men of Galilee, why do you stand gazing up into heaven? This same Jesus, who was taken up from you into heaven, will so come in like manner as you saw Him go into heaven (Ac 1:11)."

A4. Jesus Himself:
The fact that Jesus ascended to heaven is proof that He can come back again. "For the Son of Man will come in the glory of His Father with His angels, and then He will reward each according to his works (Mt 16: 27)." Indeed, Jesus unambiguously declares to His disciples that He will certainly come again. "Let not your heart be troubled; you believe in God, believe also in Me. In My Father's house are many mansions; if it were not so, I would have told you. I go to prepare a place for you. And if I go and prepare a place for you, I will come again and receive you to myself; that where I am, there you may be also (Jn 14: 1-3)."

Date Of Christ's Second Coming
It is true that Christ Himself teaches the certainty of His Second Coming. It is true that the Second Coming is part of Jesus' radical teachings. However, there is no date specified in the Bible about Christ's Second Coming. Jesus in His own words declares that the day and hour are unknown: "But of that day and hour no one knows, not even the angels of heaven, but My Father only (Mt 24: 36)." Do not let anyone fool you about any specific date; for all the previously predicted ones have failed. Setting a date is a deception designed by the Devil to prevent people from getting ready at Christ's return. Though no date is given, bear in mind that His return is certain. "Let us know, let us press on to know the LORD; his appearing is as sure as the dawn; he will come to us like the showers, like the spring rains that water the earth (Ho 6: 3)."

Signs Of Christ's Second Coming

The fact that Jesus did not give a specific date concerning His return does not undermine His teaching on this topic. He does not leave His followers in the dark either. In the Synoptic Gospels (Mt 24; Mk 13, and Lk 21) one can find many signs given by the Master that can help determine the proximity of His soon coming. Indeed, the apostle Paul in his second epistle to Timothy amplifies the list of the signs that can be viewed in the natural, political, moral, and religious world.

Signs in the Natural World:
"And there will be signs in the sun, in the moon, and in the stars; and on the earth distress of nations, with perplexity, the sea and the waves roaring (Lk 21: 25)." "And there will be famines, pestilences, and earthquakes in various places (Mt 24: 7b)." Who will forget that 2010 was declared the "Earthquakes" year? Who does not know that pestilences and hunger take the lives of many individuals daily?

Signs in the Political World:
"And you will hear of wars and rumors of wars. See that you are not troubled; for all these things must come to pass, but the end is not yet. For nation will rise against nation, and kingdom against kingdom (Mt 24: 6, 7a)." Who can nowadays ignore the reality of wars?

Signs in the Moral World:
"But know this, that in the last days perilous times will come: For men will be lovers of themselves, lovers of money, boasters, proud, blasphemers, disobedient to parents, unthankful, unholy, unloving, unforgiving, slanderers, without self-control, brutal, despisers of good, traitors, headstrong, haughty, lovers of pleasure rather than lovers of God, having a form of godliness but denying its power (2 Ti 3: 1-5)." As we look at the world in which we are living today, who can deny this convincing social reality?

Signs in the Religious World:
"For many will come in My name, saying, 'I am the Christ,' and will deceive many (Mt 24: 5)." False Christs and false prophets are on the rise these days, even among those who deny the deity of Jesus-Christ.

"And this gospel of the kingdom will be preached in all the world as a witness to all the nations, and then the end will come (Mt 24: 14)." Who could firmly foresee the gospel penetration in the European Eastern countries, such as Russia, in the 1980s? Who could imagine that Christianity would be present in some of the 1040 windows countries nowadays?

The Facts About Christ's Second Coming

It will be LITERAL:
"And when he had spoken these things, while they beheld, he was taken up; and a cloud received him out of their sight. And while looked steadfastly toward heaven as he went up, behold, two men stood by them in white apparel; which also said, 'Ye men of Galilee, why stand ye gazing up into heaven? This same Jesus, which is taken up from you into heaven, shall come in like manner as ye have seen him go into heaven'" (Ac 1: 9-11)." Luke 24: 13-49 tells us that Jesus had a real body with flesh and bones. It is worth noting that the words (beheld, sight, looked, gazing, and seen) indicate a literal scene.

It will be VISIBLE:
"Behold, He is coming with clouds, and every eye will see Him, even they who pierced Him. And all the tribes of the earth will mourn because of Him. Even so, Amen (Re 1: 7)." Every eye on earth will see him, both the wicked and the righteous. There will be no Secret Rapture. The Bible does not talk about two Second Comings, but only one. The evangelist Matthew presents the same powerful picture of visibility: "Then the sign of the Son of Man will appear in heaven, and then all the tribes of the earth will mourn, and they will see the Son of Man coming on the clouds of heaven with power and great glory (Mt 24: 30)."

It will be AUDIBLE:
"And He shall send his angels with a great sound of a trumpet, and they shall gather together his elect from the four winds, from one end of heaven to the other (Mat.24:31)." Paul reiterates these words of Jesus in his first epistle to the Thessalonians. "For the Lord Himself will descend from heaven with a shout, with the voice of an archangel, and with the trumpet of God. And the dead in Christ will rise first. Then we who are alive *and* remain shall be caught

up together with them in the clouds to meet the Lord in the air. And thus we shall always be with the Lord (1Th 4: 16, 17)." The trumpet will sound; and it will sound so loud that it will even penetrate the graves. This is again a powerful and unequivocal warning against the Secret Rapture Theory!

It will be a GLORIOUS EVENT:
"Our God shall come, and shall not keep silence: a fire shall devour before him, and it shall be tempestuous round about him (Ps.50:3)." Christ Himself describes the glorious aspect of his Second Coming: "For the Son of man shall come in the glory of his father with his angels; and then he shall reward every man according to his works (Mt 16: 27)."

It will mark the END OF THE WORLD:
"And behold, I am coming quickly, and My reward is with Me, to give to everyone according to his work (Re 22: 12)." All decisions will be made before Christ's return; there will be no second chance. Be alert to refute and denounce the Devilish Secret Rapture Theory!

The Purposes Of Christ's Second Coming
Among several other reasons, Christ will come back in order to:

a. **Gather the chosen.** "And He will send His angels with a great sound of a trumpet, and they will gather together His elect from the four winds, from one end of heaven to the other (Mt 24: 31)."

b. **Bring the dead in Christ to life.** "For the Lord Himself will descend from heaven with a shout, with the voice of an archangel, and with the trumpet of God. And the dead in Christ will rise first (1Th 4: 16)."

c. **To transform and receive all the saints.** "Behold, I tell you a mystery: We shall not all sleep, but we shall all be changed in a moment, in the twinkling of an eye, at the last trumpet. For the trumpet will sound, and the dead will be raised incorruptible, and we shall be changed (1 Co 15:51, 52)." See also Philippians 3: 21.

d. **Seek and take his people home.** "In My Father's house are many mansions; if it were not so, I would have told you. I go to prepare a place for you. And if I go and prepare a place for you, I will come again and receive you to Myself; that where I am, there you may be also (John 14:2, 3)." See also 1 Thes.4: 17.

e. **Judge the world.** "I charge you therefore before God and the Lord Jesus Christ, who will judge the living and the dead at His appearing and His kingdom (2 Ti 4: 1)." See also John 5: 28, 29.

f. **Give the kingdom to his people.** "Then the kingdom and dominion, and the greatness of the kingdoms under the whole heaven, shall be given to the people, the saints of the Most High. His kingdom *is* an everlasting kingdom, and all dominions shall serve and obey Him (Da 7: 27)."

Only Two Groups At Jesus' Return

Make no mistake about it; Christ is coming again. At His return, there will be only two groups of people (the unjust and filthy living and dead, and the just and holy living and dead). "He who is unjust, let him be unjust still; he who is filthy, let him be filthy still; he who is righteous, let him be righteous still; he who is holy, let him be holy still (Re 22:11)."

The seer of Patmos, on one hand, portrays the anguish of the first group as follows: "Then the sky receded as a scroll when it is rolled up, and every mountain and island was moved out of its place. And the kings of the earth, the great men, the rich men, the commanders, the mighty men, every slave and every free man, hid themselves in the caves and in the rocks of the mountains, and said to the mountains and rocks, "Fall on us and hide us from the face of Him who sits on the throne and from the wrath of the Lamb! For the great day of His wrath has come, and who is able to stand?" (Re 6: 14-17)?"

The prophet Isaiah, on the other hand, describes with great anticipation the joy of the second group on the twenty-fifth chapter of his book: "And it will be said in that day: ""Behold, this is our God; we have waited for Him, and He will save us. This is the LORD; we have waited for Him; we will be glad and rejoice in His salvation" (Is 25: 9)."

Dear friend, the Second Coming of Jesus Christ is not a fable, nor a myth but a reality. It is true that heaven is beyond comprehension, but it is a reality. In John 14:1-3, Jesus promised each a mansion that He has prepared. Our sinful minds cannot comprehend the beauty and glory of our heavenly home, but it is reality. Would you like to be there to enjoy eternity with Jesus? Are you ready to go with him? Jesus is knocking at the door of your heart right now; do you want to let Him in? Which one of these two groups are you planning to join? I urge you to select the second. Knowing there are two groups is one thing; however, being part of the loving and obedient group (Jn 15: 14) that has a good relationship with Jesus is very crucial. It is up to you to make the right choice. See also Revelation 12: 17 and 14:12.

Realities About Christ's Second Coming

The Good News about Christ's return is that the Second Coming is certain. Jesus says that He will come back again. "And if I go and prepare a place for you, I will come again and receive you to Myself; that where I am, there you may be also (Jn 14: 3)."

The Bad News about Christ's soon return is that some people unfortunately will not be ready. "Not everyone who says to Me, 'Lord, Lord,' shall enter the kingdom of heaven, but he who does the will of My Father in heaven (Mt 7:21)." See also Matthew 25: 11, 12

The Most Important News about Christ's Second Coming is to be ready. "Therefore you also be ready, for the Son of Man is coming at an hour you do not expect (Mt 24:44)."

I am glad you asked how you can get ready. The simple way to be ready is to know Jesus (Jn 17: 3) and accept Him as your personal Savior. The most important decision is to be ready. And to be ready at His coming you need to be ready today. Would you like to enjoy eternity with Jesus? Join the second group right now. Do not say or think you will have time to do so in the future. "Come now, you who say, 'Today or tomorrow we will go to such and such a city, spend a year there, buy and sell, and make a profit;' whereas you do not know what will happen tomorrow. For what is your life? It is even a vapor that appears for a little time and then vanishes away (Ja 4: 13, 14)."

Christ loves you, wants to save you, and is preparing a place for you. Just say "Yes" to Him and you will never regret having made such an important decision in your life. God bless you and be ready for Christ's soon Second Coming, the greatest and ultimate comeback!

APPENDIX

APPENDIX A

NAME OF SELECTED CHURCH
DISCIPLESHIP SEMINAR: APRIL 12 – JUNE 21, 2014
ACTIVE PARTICIPANT CONSENT FORM

Name:_____ & Phone:

Are you a baptized member of the church?   Yes [ ]   No [ ]
I have been baptized for less than 2 years.   Yes [ ]   No [ ]
Gender: Female [ ]   Male [ ]
Age Group: 16-20 [ ], 21-29 [ ], 30 -39 [ ], 40+ [ ]

1. I will do my best to attend the 10 sessions of this seminar.   Yes [ ] No [ ]
2. I will give my full participation in all the activities.   Yes [ ] No [ ]
3. I will treat each individual with a godly respect.   Yes [ ] No [ ]
4. I will do and submit my assignment on a timely basis.   Yes [ ] No [ ]
5. I will keep all confidential information secret.   Yes [ ] No [ ]
6. I will behave accordingly with the established rules.   Yes [ ] No [ ]
7. I am attending this seminar to know more about Jesus.   Yes [ ] No [ ]
8. I promise to share my knowledge of Jesus with others.   Yes [ ] No [ ]

The seminar is held in a Christian environment. Any misconduct will prevent me from attending part or all the presentations.

Print your name here: Sign your name here:

Date:

APPENDIX B

PRE & POST-TEST QUESTIONS
(With slight modification in some post-test questions)

Instructions I: Your understanding of the concept of discipleship. For each of the following statements, choose the answers that best describe your thoughts.

SD = Strongly Disagree; D = Disagree; N =Neutral;
A = Agree; SA = Strongly Agree.

[1]. Discipleship is a passionate desire to follow Jesus and lead others to Him as well.
SD ( )   D ( )   N ( )   A ( )   SA ( )

[2]. The Gospel commission indicates that the basic mission of the church is to make disciples.
SD ( )   D ( )   N ( )   A ( )   SA ( )

[3]. The goal of every disciple is to become like Jesus.
SD ( )   D ( )   N ( )   A ( )   SA ( )

[4]. I want to be an authentic disciple of Jesus Christ.
SD ( )   D ( )   N ( )   A ( )   SA ( )

Instructions II: Basic elements of discipleship (Love, Understanding, Ministering, Equipping).

For each of the following statements, choose the answers that best describe your thoughts.

[5]. I am attracted by programs that draw me closer to Christ and help me develop a deeper loving relationship with God.
SD ( )   D ( )   N ( )   A ( )   SA ( )

[6]. It is critical to me to demonstrate love and kindness to all people.

SD ( )   D ( )   N ( )   A ( )   SA ( )

[7]. Spending quality time in prayer to God becomes my top priority.

SD ( )   D ( )   N ( )   A ( )   SA ( )

[8]. God's love to me is unconditional even when I transgress His Law.

SD ( )   D ( )   N ( )   A ( )   SA ( )

[9]. It is convincing to me that the church is God's agency on earth, a community of faith where I can grow spiritually.

SD ( )   D ( )   N ( )   A ( )   SA ( )

[10]. My body is the temple of God. I feel greatly responsible for its care.

SD ( )   D ( )   N ( )   A ( )   SA ( )

[11]. Not long after baptism, I have started to share my new faith with others.

SD ( )   D ( )   N ( )   A ( )   SA ( )

[12]. I feel now more steadfast to help those who are in need.

SD ( )   D ( )   N ( )   A ( )   SA ( )

[13]. I have sometimes tried to lead someone to Christ after my conversion.

SD ( )   D ( )   N ( )   A ( )   SA ( )

[14]. My spiritual mentor has greatly helped me build up my religious faith.

SD ( )   D ( )   N ( )   A ( )   SA ( )

[15]. Worshipping the Lord in family has deepened my relationship with God.

SD ( )   D ( )   N ( )   A ( )   SA ( )

[16]. It is crucial to me to be around friends who regularly attend religious services.

SD ( )   D ( )   N ( )   A ( )   SA ( )

APPENDIX C

FORMAT SAMPLE TOPIC PRESENTATION
EXAMPLE: PRAYER and DISCIPLESHIP

1. CLIMATE CONTROL GUIDE
    a. Organizational Climate (Arrange for small group relationships and learning).
    b. Social Climate (Help participants be comfortable to share their experiences).
    c. Climate for doing learning tasks (Help participants be positive in accomplishing their learning goals).

2. GENERAL DESIRED OUTCOMES:
    a. Knowledge: Upon successful completion of the presentation, participants will understand that a disciple cannot live without prayer.
    b. Skills and Behaviors: Upon completion of the workshop, participants will be able to pray properly, lead a group in a prayer meeting.
    c. Attitudes, Values, Commitments: Upon completion of the workshop, participants will make a commitment to develop a lifestyle of prayer.

3. SPECIFIC DESIRED OUTCOMES:
    A. Knowledge: Upon completion of this presentation, the participants will
        a. be able to define prayer as per the biblical understanding,
        b. know how prayer is a tool of communication,
        c. know that God answers personal prayer,
        d. be assured that God responds to collective prayer, and
        e. understand that prayer is a continuous activity. Know that Jesus values prayer.

B. Skills and Behaviors: Upon completion of this workshop, participants will

    f. feel the necessity of prayer,

    g. be able to share their prayer experiences with others,

    h. pray to God with conviction and assurance, and

    i. feel that it is normal to pray without ceasing.

C. Attitudes, Values, Commitments: After this seminar, participants will

    j. value the importance of prayer,

    k. commit themselves to leading a life of prayer,

    l. pray before making an important decision, and

    m. commit themselves to pray for others.

STRATEGY:

1. **Devotion**

2. *Telling:* Welcome the participants and give ground for this workshop is taken place.

3. *Illustration::* Ask each person to hold their breathing for about 3 to 5 minutes…

4. *Ice-breaker:* Have each participant look for a partner and greet each other.

5. *Discussion 1:* Each participant gives a definition of prayer in their small group panel.

6. *Presentation:* Notes and Power Point – We are all disciples of Jesus. We are supposed to reproduce what He did. His entire life was a life of prayer. When He woke up in the morning, the first thing He did was communicate to his Father (Mark 1:35). Prayer occupied every aspect of His ministry, for He was constantly in contact with God through prayer. Not only did He teach his disciples how to pray, but he also gave them reasons to pray (Luke 11:9-13), and particularly told them not to fall into temptation (Mat.26:41). If we need food to keep our physical body in good shape, we need prayer as well to keep our spiritual self in good shape. If Jesus, who never sinned, spent so much time in prayer, it is more than necessary for us to set time aside for prayer. As disciples, let us follow Jesus' habit (Luke 5:16).

7. *Discussion 2:* Read in groups about three different modes of prayer (Dominical in Matthew 6, Confession in Psalm 51, and Intercession in John 17). Have each participant share their personal experiences of prayer. Conclude with a series of prayers, two by two.

8. **Questions and Answers**

9. *Commitment:* Each participant chooses a partner and engages to pray for them.

10. *Wrap-up:* summarize what we have seen so far.

- When we pray to God, we develop an intimacy with Him (Love).
- When we pray, we understand better the Word of God (understanding)
- When we pray for others (ministering), we want good for them.
- When we pray, the Holy Spirit prepares (equipping) us for a better ministry.

11. Closing prayer and reminder of assignment (Assessment or Participants' Evaluation).

APPENDIX D

ASSESSMENT FORM (SAMPLE)

Instructions:

For each of the following statements, circle the numbers that best describe your thoughts.

> SD = Strongly Disagree; D = Disagree; N =Neutral;
> A = Agree; SA = Strongly Agree

Outcome Assessment

1. This presentation helped me discover that prayer is a tool of communication with God.

SD ( )	D ( )	N ( )	A ( )	SA ( )
1	2	3	4	5

2. I am now more reliable to share my prayer experiences with others.

SD ( )	D ( )	N ( )	A ( )	SA ( )
1	2	3	4	5

3. I am committed myself to pray for others.

SD ( )	D ( )	N ( )	A ( )	SA ( )
1	2	3	4	5

4. I will make plan to attend all the other presentations.

SD ( )	D ( )	N ( )	A ( )	SA ( )
1	2	3	4	5

Any comments:

APPENDIX E

PARTICIPANTS OVERALL PERFORMANCE
PRE & POST-TEST Part I

Table 1: Results to [1]. Discipleship is a passionate desire to follow Jesus and lead others to him as well.

	PRE-TEST %		POST-TEST %	
Number of Participants	18	100	18	100
Strongly Disagree	3	17	0	0
Disagree	4	22	0	0
Neutral	2	11	1	5
Agree	8	44	7	39
Strongly Agree	1	06	10	56

Table 2: Results to [2]. The Gospel commission indicates that the basic mission of the church is to make disciples.

	PRE-TEST %		POST-TEST %	
Number of Participants	18	100	18	100
Strongly Disagree	4	22	0	0
Disagree	2	11	0	0
Neutral	1	6	1	6
Agree	9	50	5	28
Strongly Agree	2	11	12	66

Table 3: Results to [3]. The goal of every disciple is to become like Jesus.

	PRE-TEST	%	POST-TEST	%
Number of Participants	18	100	18	100
Strongly Disagree	3	17	0	0
Disagree	2	11	0	0
Neutral	5	28	0	0
Agree	6	33	5	28
Strongly Agree	2	11	13	72

Table 4: Results to [4]. I want to be an authentic disciple of Jesus Christ.

	PRE-TEST	%	POST-TEST	%
Number of Participants	18	100	18	100
Strongly Disagree	1	6	0	0
Disagree	3	16	0	0
Neutral	1	6	1	6
Agree	9	50	5	28
Strongly Agree	4	22	12	66

PRE & POST-TEST Part II

Table 5: Results to 5. I am attracted by programs that draw me closer to Christ and help me develop a deeper loving relationship with God.

	PRE-TEST	%	POST-TEST	%
Number of Participants	18	100	18	100
Strongly Disagree	1	6	0	0
Disagree	3	16	0	0
Neutral	0	0	0	0
Agree	4	22	2	11
Strongly Agree	10	56	16	89

Table 6: Results to 6. It is critical to me to demonstrate love and kindness to all people.

	PRE-TEST	%	POST-TEST	%
Number of Participants	18	100	18	100
Strongly Disagree	1	6	0	0
Disagree	3	16	1	6
Neutral	3	17	1	6
Agree	9	50	9	50
Strongly Agree	2	11	7	38

Table 7: Results to 7. Spending quality time in prayer to God becomes my top priority.

	PRE-TEST	%	POST-TEST	%
Number of Participants	18	100	18	100
Strongly Disagree	0	0	0	0
Disagree	0	0	0	0
Neutral	2	11	1	5
Agree	6	33	1	6
Strongly Agree	10	56	16	89

Table 8: Results to 8. God's love to me is unconditional even when I transgress His Law.

	PRE-TEST	%	POST-TEST	%
Number of Participants	18	100	18	100
Strongly Disagree	8	44	0	0
Disagree	3	17	0	0
Neutral	1	5	1	6
Agree	5	28	2	11
Strongly Agree	1	6	15	83

Table 9: Results to [9]. It is convincing to me that the church is God's agency on earth, a community of faith where I can grow spiritually.

	PRE-TEST	%	POST-TEST	%
Number of Participants	18	100	18	100
Strongly Disagree	1	5	0	0
Disagree	3	17	0	0
Neutral	1	6	1	6
Agree	7	39	6	33
Strongly Agree	6	33	11	61

Table 10: Results to 10. My body is the temple of God. I feel greatly responsible for its care.

	PRE-TEST	%	POST-TEST	%
Number of Participants	18	100	18	100
Strongly Disagree	0	0	0	0
Disagree	0	0	0	0
Neutral	2	11	0	0
Agree	10	56	6	33
Strongly Agree	6	33	12	67

Table 11: Results to 11. Not long after baptism, I have started to share my new faith with other people.

	PRE-TEST	%	POST-TEST	%
Number of Participants	18	100	18	100
Strongly Disagree	2	11	0	0
Disagree	10	56	0	0
Neutral	1	5	2	11
Agree	5	28	3	17
Strongly Agree	0	0	13	72

Table 12: Results to 12. I feel now more steadfast to help those who are in need.

	PRE-TEST	%	POST-TEST	%
Number of Participants	18	100	18	100
Strongly Disagree	2	11	0	0
Disagree	5	28	0	0
Neutral	1	6	1	5
Agree	8	44	5	28
Strongly Agree	2	11	12	67

Table 13: Results to 13. I have sometimes tried to lead someone to Christ after my conversion.

	PRE-TEST	%	POST-TEST	%
Number of Participants	18	100	18	100
Strongly Disagree	5	28	0	0
Disagree	7	39	0	0
Neutral	0	0	2	11
Agree	5	28	3	17
Strongly Agree	1	5	13	72

Table 14: Results to 14. Church leadership has greatly helped me build up my religious faith.

	PRE-TEST	%	POST-TEST	%
Number of Participants	18	100	18	100
Strongly Disagree	0	0	0	0
Disagree	0	0	0	0
Neutral	1	6	0	0
Agree	2	11	2	11
Strongly Agree	15	83	16	89

Table 15: Results to 15. Family devotion has considerably helped me deepen my relationship with God.

	PRE-TEST	%	POST-TEST	%
Number of Participants	18	100	18	100
Strongly Disagree	0	0	0	0
Disagree	1	6	0	0
Neutral	2	11	1	6
Agree	3	16	0	0
Strongly Agree	12	67	17	94

Table 16: Results to 16. It is crucial to me to be around friends who regularly attend religious services.

	PRE-TEST	%	POST-TEST	%
Number of Participants	18	100	18	100
Strongly Disagree	0	0	0	0
Disagree	1	6	0	0
Neutral	3	16	0	0
Agree	1	6	2	11
Strongly Agree	13	72	16	89

Table 17 – Data Triangulation

Categories	Coding		Questionnaire	700 Word Essay	Interviews
Love	L		16/18 or 89%	8/10 or 80%	7/8 or 88%
Understanding	U		15/18 or 83%	7/10 or 70%	6/8 or 75%
Ministering	M		13/18 or 72%	7/10 or 70%	6/8 or 75%
Equipping	E		17/18 or 94%	9/10 or 90%	8/8 or 100%
Networking	N	N/A	16/16 or 100%	10/10 or 100%	8/8 or 100%

L (Loving): Love for God and fellow human beings.

U (Understanding): Understanding the Word of God.

M (Ministering): Witnessing through evangelism and service.

E (Equipping): Being equipped for a more effective witnessing.

N (Networking): Making new friends, fellowship and sharing: established and being developed throughout the seminar.*

*Only one question has been asked about Networking in the beginning of the seminar: Do you want to make new friends? The response has been yes for all.

LUMEN: Sharing the Light of the Word with each other through calling, texting, and e-mailing.

APPENDIX F

Based on what you have learned on these four characteristics (Love, Understanding the Word of God, Ministering, and Equipping) of discipleship during the seminar, please answer the following questions:

1. Why are you attracted to programs that draw you closer to Christ and help you develop a deeper loving relationship with God?
2. Why and how critical is it to you to demonstrate love and kindness to all people?
3. Why does spending quality time in prayer to God become your top priority?
4. How do you know that God still loves you even when you transgress His Law?
5. Why should you feel responsible for taking care of your body?
6. Why have you started sharing with others your new faith right after baptism?
7. Why and how often do you help others with their problems?
8. How often and why have you tried to lead someone to Christ?
9. How much and why do you think that training is important to you?
10. Why and how has your family helped you in your relationship with God?

APPENDIX G

QUESTIONNAIRE

Instructions II: Basic elements of discipleship (Love, Understanding, Ministering, Equipping).

On a scale of 1 to 5 (1 being the weakest and 5 the strongest), how do you answer the following questions?

1. How attracted are you by programs that draw you closer to Christ and help you develop a deeper loving relationship with God?

    1 ( )   2 ( )   3 ( )   4 ( )   5 ( )

2. How critical is it to you to demonstrate love and kindness to all people?

    1 ( )   2 ( )   3 ( )   4 ( )   5 ( )

3. Why does spending quality time in prayer to God become your top priority in life?

    1 ( )   2 ( )   3 ( )   4 ( )   5 ( )

4. How sure are you that you are loved by God even when you transgress His Law?

    1 ( )   2 ( )   3 ( )   4 ( )   5 ( )

5. How convincing is it to you that the church is God's agency on earth, a community of faith where you can grow spiritually and experience love and fellowship?

    1 ( )   2 ( )   3 ( )   4 ( )   5 ( )

6. Your body is the temple of God. Do you really feel responsible for its care?

1 ( )   2 ( )   3 ( )   4 ( )   5 ( )

7. How often after your conversion have you told others about God's goodness toward you?

1 ( )   2 ( )   3 ( )   4 ( )   5 ( )

8. When have you realized that helping others is important and how often do you do that?

1 ( )   2 ( )   3 ( )   4 ( )   5 ( )

9. How often after your conversion have you tried to lead someone to Christ?

1 ( )   2 ( )   3 ( )   4 ( )   5 ( )

10. How much has the church leadership helped you build up your religious faith?

1 ( )   2 ( )   3 ( )   4 ( )   5 ( )

11. How much has family devotion helped you deepen your relationship with God?

1 ( )   2 ( )   3 ( )   4 ( )   5 ( )

12. How vital is it to you to be around friends who regularly attend religious services?

1 ( )   2 ( )   3 ( )   4 ( )   5 ( )

APPENDIX H

THEME SONG

"Seeking the Lost"

I

Seeking the lost-yes, kindly entreating
Wanderers on the mountain astray
"Come unto Me," His message repeating,
Words of the Master speaking today

Chorus

Going afar upon the mountain,
Bringing the wand'rer back again,
Into the fold of my Redeemer,
Jesus the Lamb for sinners slain.

II

Seeking the lost-and pointing to Jesus
Souls that are weak and hearts that are sore,
Leading them forth in ways of salvation,
Showing the path to life evermore.

APPENDIX I

NAME OF THE CHURCH
DEPARTMENT OF PERSONAL MINISTRIES
CERTIFICATE OF COMPLETION

This certificate is granted to _____ for having
successfully completed a 20-hour class for the course:

"INTRODUCTION TO DISCIPLESHIP"
Class duration: April 12, 2014 – June 21, 2014.

_____

Dr. SO, D.Min., Senior Pastor

_____

Dr. Benoit Petit-Homme, Instructor

Date:

ENDNOTES

i Survey of Former & Inactive Adventist Church Members, conducted for the Office of Archives, Statistics and Research, General Conference of Seventh-day Adventists by the Center for Creative Ministry 2013, can be accessed for full reading at adventistarchives.org , or write to Center for Creative Ministry @ Milton Freewater, Oregon 97862 (www.creativeministry.org), Paul Richardson, Project Manager.

ii This definition is taken from Power Point presentations for the course Field Evangelism Preaching. The Purpose of Public Evangelism, Chapter one, Reaping the Harvest by Dr. Ron Clouzet, Andrews University, Spring Semester, 2010.

iii This quotation from the book, The Ministry of Healing by Ellen G. White, p.143, due to its importance in regard to reach the unsaved for Christ, has been cited twice in this manual in order to put emphasis on the technique to do evangelism like the Master, Jesus, did.

BIBLIOGRAPHY

Ammerman, Nancy T., Jackson W. Carroll, Carl S. Dudley and William McKinney, eds. *Studying Congregations: A New Handbook*. Nashville, TN: Abingdon Press, 1998.

Ayling, Stanley. *John Wesley*. New York, NY: William Collins Publishing, Inc., 1979.

Bell, Skip. *Servants & Friends, A Biblical Theology of Leadership*. Berrien Springs, MI: Andrews University Press, 2014.

Blazen, Ivan T, ed. *Handbook of Seventh-day Adventist Theology*. Edited by George W. Reid, Commentary Reference. Hagerstown, MD: Review and Herald Publishing Association, 2000.

Blomberg, Craig L. *The New American Commentary, Vol.22 Matthew*. Nashville, TN: Broadman & Holman Publishers, 1992.

Bonhoeffer, Dietrich. *The Cost of Discipleship*. New York, NY: Touchstone, 1995.

Borgen, Ole E. *John Wesley on the Sacraments*. Zurich, Switzerland: Publishing House of the United Methodist Church, 1972.

Buttrick, George Arthur. *The Interpreter's Bible*. Nashville, TN: Abingdon Press, 1980.

Carter, Charles W., ed. *A Contemporary Wesleyan Theology*. Vol. 2. Grand Rapids, MI: Francis Asbury Press, 1983.

Childs, Brevard S. *The Book of Exodus: A Critical, Theological Commentary*. Philadelphia, PA: The Westminster Press, 1974.

Clapper, Gregory S. *The Renewal of the Heart Is the Mission of the Church:*

Wesley's Heart Religion in the Twenty-First Century. Eugene, OR: Cascade Books, 2010.

Clements, Ronald E. *The Cambridge Bible Commentary: Exodus*. London, UK: Cambridge University Press, 1972.

Cloud, Dr. Henry and Dr. John Townsend. *How People Grow: What the Bible Reveals About Personal Growth*. Grand Rapids, MI: Zondervan, 2001.

Cole, R. Denis. *Numbers: The New American Commentary*. Vol. 3B Nashville, TN: Broadman &Holman Publishers, 2000.

Cranton, Patricia. *Professional Development as Transformative Learning: New Perspectives for Teachers of Adults*. San Francisco, CA: Jossey-Bass, 1996.

Cress, James A. *Common Sense Ministry Multiplied*. Nampa, ID: Pacific Press Publishing Association, 2010.

Creswell, John W. *Research Design: Qualitative, Quantitative, and Mixed Methods Approaches*. Thousand Oaks, CA: SAGEPublications, Inc., 2009.

Dederen, Raoul, ed. *Handbook of Seventh-day Adventist Theology*. Edited by George W. Reid, Commentary Reference. Hagerstown, MD: Review and Herald Publishing Association, 2000.

Diop, Ganoune. *Make Disciples: The Art of Moving Beyond Conversion to a Passion for Christ*. Huntsville, AL: Oakwood College Press, 2010.

Dunavant, Del. *From Membership to Discipleship: A Practical Guide to Equipping Members for Ministry*. Lincoln, NE: AdventSource, 2006.

Elleingsen, Mark. *Reclaiming Our Root: An Inclusive Introduction to Church History*, Vol. II. Harrisburg, PA: Trinity Press International, 1999.

Elwell, Walter A. *Evangelical Dictionary of Theology, 2nd Ed*. Grand Rapids, MI: Baker Academic, 2001.

Enns, Peter. *Exodus: The NIV Application Commentary*. Grand Rapids, MI: Zondervan Publishing House, 2000.

Finley, Mark and Ernestine. *Fulfilling God's End-Time Mission: A Comprehensive Evangelism Training Manual*. Nampa, ID: Pacific Press Publishing Association, 2013.

Fowler, James W. *Stages of Faith: The Psychology of Human Development and the Quest for Meaning*. New York, NY: Harper One, 1981.

Fretheim, Terence E. *Exodus Interpretation: A Bible Commentary for Teaching and Preaching.* Louisville, KY: John Knox Press, 1991.

Gill, Frederic C. *Selected Letters of John Wesley.* New York, NY: The Philosophical Library, Inc., 1956.

Guinness, Os. *The Call: Finding and Fulfilling the Central Purpose of Your Life.* Nashville, TN: Thomas Nelson, 2003.

Hawkins, Thomas R. *Cultivating Christian Community.* Nashville, TN: Discipleship Resources, 2001.

Heath, Gordon L. *Doing Church History: A User-Friendly Introduction to Researching the History of Christianity.* Toronto, Canada: Clements Publishing, 2008.

Hendel, Kurt K. "No Salvation Outside the Church in Light of Luther's Dialectic of the Hidden and Revealed God." *Currents in Theology and Mission,* (2008).

Hendricks, Howard. *Teaching to Change Lives: Seven Proven Ways to Make Your Teaching Come Alive.* Sisters, OR: Multnomah Publishers, 1987.

Jones, Scott J. *The Evangelistic Love of God & Neighbor: A Theology of Witness & Discipleship.* Nashville, TN: Abingdon Press, 2003.

Kidder, S. Joseph. *The Big Four: Secrets to a Thriving Church Family.* Hagerstown, MD: Review and Herald Publishing Association, 2011.

Macchia, Stephen A. *Becoming a Healthy Disciple: Ten Traits of a Vital Christian.* Grand Rapids, MI: Baker Books, 2004.

Mallory, Sue. *The Equipping Church: Serving Together to Transform Lives.* Grand Rapids, MI: Zondervan Publishing House, 1994.

Malphurs, Aubrey. *Strategic Disciple Making: A Practical Tool for Successful Ministry.* Grand Rapids, MI: Baker Books, 2009.

Mann, Thomas. *The Oxford Guide to Library Research: How to Find Reliable Information Online and Offline.* Third ed. New York, NY: Oxford University Press, 2005.

Matthaei, Sondra Higgins. *Making Disciple: Faith Formation in the Wesleyan Tradition.* Nashville, TN: Abingdon Press, 2000.

Maxwell, John C. *The 21 Indispensable Qualities of a Leader: Becoming the Person Others Will Want to Follow.* Nashville, TN: Thomas Nelson, 1999.

McBride, Neal F. *How to Have Great Small-Group Meetings.* Colorado Springs, CO: NAVPRESS, 1997.

McCallun, Dennis and Jessica Lowery. *Organic Disciplemaking*. Houston, TX: Touch Publications, 2006.

McIntosh, Gary and Glen Martin. *Finding Them, Keeping Them: Effective Strategies for Evangelism and Assimilation in the Local Church*. Nashville, TN: B & H Publishing Group, 1992.

Miller, William R. and Kathleen A. Jackson. *Practical Psychology for Pastors*. Eugene, OR: Wipf & Stock Publishers, 2010.

Moore, Ralph. *Making Disciples: Developing Lifelong Followers of Jesus*. Ventura, CA: Regal, 2012.

Morgan, David L. *Focus Groups as Qualitative Research*. Second ed. Thousand Oaks, CA: SAGE Publications, Inc., 1997.

Morley, Patrick. *No Man Left Behind: How to Build and Sustain a Thriving, Disciple-Making Ministry for Every Man of Your Church*. Chicago, IL: Moody Publishers, 2006.

Morneau, Roger J. *When You Need Incredible Answers to Prayer*. Hagerstown, MD: Review and Herald Publishing Association, 1995.

Munroe, Myles. *Understanding Your Potential: Discovering the Hidden You*. Shippensburg, PA: Destiny Image Publishers, 2002.

Myers, Bryant L. *Walking with the Poor: Principles and Practices of Transformational Development*. Maryknoll, NY: Orbis Books, 2009.

Oden, Thomas C. *John Wesley's Scriptural Christianity*. Grand Rapids, MI: Zondervan Publishing House, 1994.

Ogden, Greg. *Unfinished Business: Returning the Ministry to the People of God*. Grand Rapids, MI: Zondervan, 2003.

Rainer, Tom S. *Simple Church: Returning to God's Process for Making Disciples*. Nashville, TN: B&H Publishing Group, 2006.

Ralph W. Neighbour, Jr. *Where Do We Go from Here?: A Guidebook for the Cell Group Church*. Houston, Texas: Touch Publications, 2000.

Samaan, Philip G. *Christ's Way of Making Disciples*. Hagerstown, MD: Review and Herald Publishing Association, 1999.

Samaan, Philip G. *Christ's Method Alone*. Hagerstown, MD: Review and Herald Publishing Association, 2012.

Sider, Ronald J. *Good News and Good Works: A Theology of the Whole Gospel*. Grand Rapids, MI: Baker Books, 1983.

Simson, Wolfgang. *Houses That Change the World: The Return of the House*

Churches. Waynesboro, GA: Authentic, 2001.

Smither, Edward. "'To Emulate and Imitate:' Possidius' Life of Augustine as a Fifth Century Discipleship Tool." *Southwestern Journal of Theology*, no. discipleship, (2008).

Solis, Dan. "Discipleship: Adult Sabbath School Bible Study Guide," In *Sabbath School Personal Ministries*, edited by Seventh-day Adventist Church. Nampa, ID: Pacific Press Publishing Association, 2014.

Spader, Dann and Gary Mayes. *Growing a Healthy Church*. Chicago, IL: Moody Press, 1991.

Speidel, Royal. *Evangelism in the Small Membership Church*. Nashville, TN: Abingdon Press, 2007.

Bryant Sr., Donald Earl. "Retaining and Engaging Members in the Life of the Congregation." United Theological Seminary, 2007.

Steger, Carlos. "The Teachings of Jesus: Adult Sabbath School Study Guide." In *Sabbath School Personal Ministries*, edited by Seventh-day Adventist Church. Nampa, ID: Pacific Press Publishing Association, 2014.

Stott, John R. W. *The Message of Acts: The Spirit, the Church, and the World*. Downers Grove, IL: Inter-Varsity Press, 1994.

Stuart, Douglas K. *Exodus: The New American Commentary*, Vol. II. Nashville, TN: Broadman &Holman Publishers, 2006.

Sugden, Edward H. *John Wesley's Fifty-Three Sermons*. Nashville, TN: Abingdon Press, 1983.

Thayer, Jane. "Teaching for Discipleship: Strategies for Transformational Learning." 2009.

Thomas, Owen C. and Ellen K. Wondra. *Introduction to Theology*, 3rd ed. Harrisburg, PA: MoreHouse Publishing, 2002.

Thomas, Terry. *Becoming a Fruit-Bearing Disciple*. Raleigh, NC: Voice of Rehoboth Publishing, 2005.

Thorp, Karen Lee. *How to Ask Great Questions: Guide Your Group to Discovery with These Proven Techniques*. Colorado Springs, CO: NavPress, 1998.

Tiffany, Frederick C. and Sharon H. Ringe. *Biblical Interpretation: A Roadmap*. Nashville, TN: Abingdon Press, 1996.

Vickers, Jason E. *Minding the Good Ground: A Theology for Church Renewal*.

Waco, TX: Baylor University Press, 2011.

Vyhmeister, Jean. *Your Indispensible Guide to Writing Quality Research Papers for Students of Religion and Theology*. Grand Rapids, MI: Zondervan Publishing House, 2001.

Warren, Rick. *The Purpose Driven Church*. Grand Rapids, MI: Zondervan Publishing House, 1995.

White, Ellen G. *The Ministry of Healing*. Nampa, ID: Pacific Press Publishing Association, 2003.

White, Ellen G. *Evangelism*. Washington, D.C.: Review and Herald Publishing Association, 1946.

White, Ellen G. *Christian Service*. Hagerstown: Review and Herald Publishing Association, 2002.

White, Ellen G. *In Heavenly Places*. Hagerstown: Review and Herald Publishing Association, 1995.

Wilson, Marlene. *How to Mobilize Church Volunteers*. Minneapolis, MN: Augsburg Publishing House, 1983.

THANK YOU

It would be very difficult, even impossible, to bring this book to completion all by myself. Thus, I want those who have given their contributions (tangible or intangible) to know that they have been highly appreciated. The list is very long. Since I do not want to miss anyone, I refrain myself from citing names. You know yourselves, don't you? Please be reminded that this page is dedicated to all of you!

However, there is no rule without exception; I am delighted to address a special 'Thank You' to Dr. JUNIAS DESAMOUR, MD / INTERNAL MEDICINE for his sponsorship through:

OMNI MEDICAL CLINIC
425 S. Hunt Club Blvd Suite 2001
Apopka, FL 32703
P: 407.705.3636   /   F: 407.809.5222

Once again, thank you to all!

The author,
Dr. Benoit Petit-Homme, D.Min